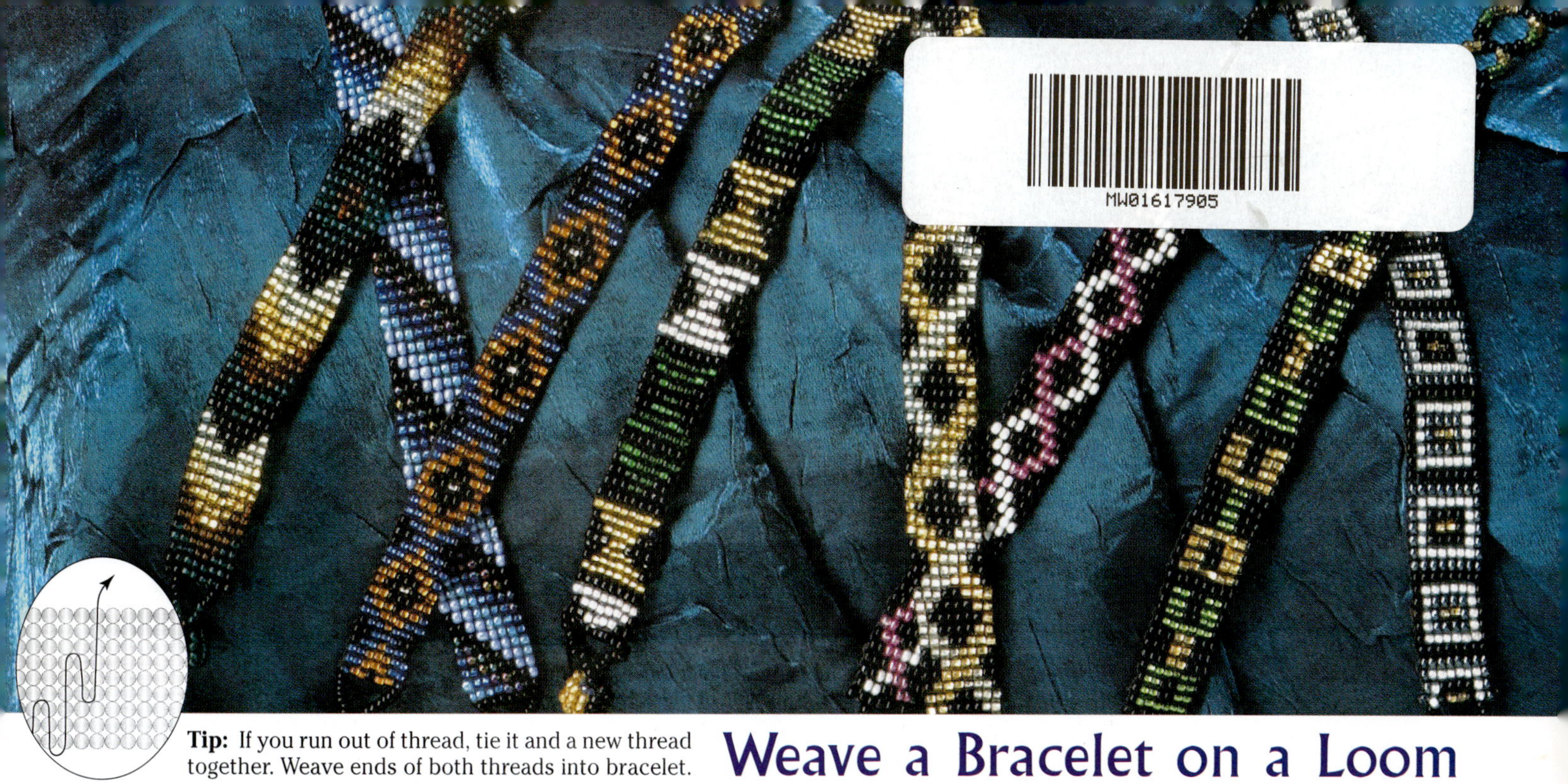

Tip: If you run out of thread, tie it and a new thread together. Weave ends of both threads into bracelet.

Weave a Bracelet on a Loom

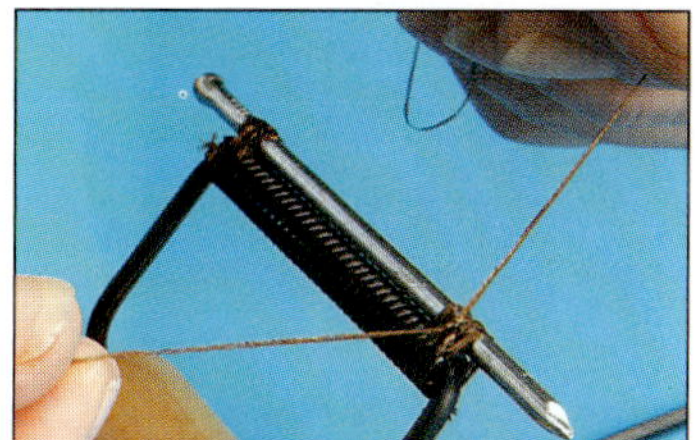

1. To convert a regular bead loom for bracelets, tie a 3½" finishing nail on each end of the loom. Tie a thread (called the warp thread) to loom, leaving a 10" tail.

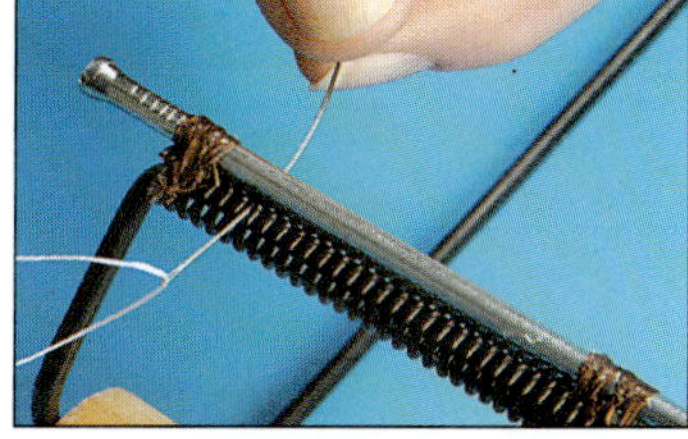

2 Thread a needle and begin to warp the loom. You will need to pass the needle BETWEEN the coil on the loom and the nail. Wrap 9 threads (for bracelet on page 2).

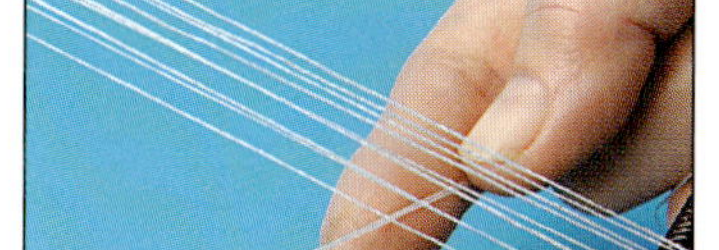

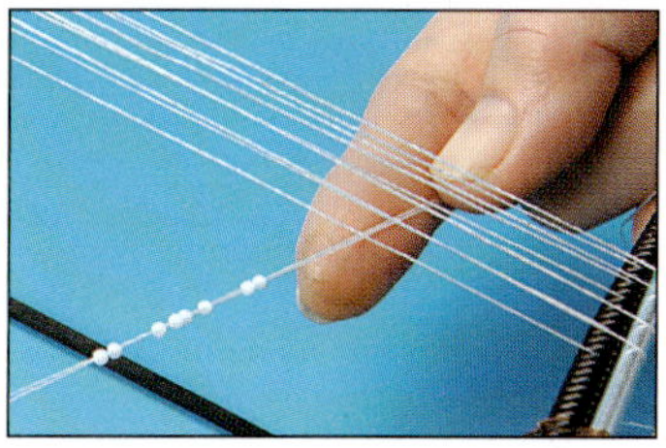

3. Begin to weave the first row with beads. Thread 8 beads (for bracelet on page 2) then position the thread and beads to go UNDER the warp threads.

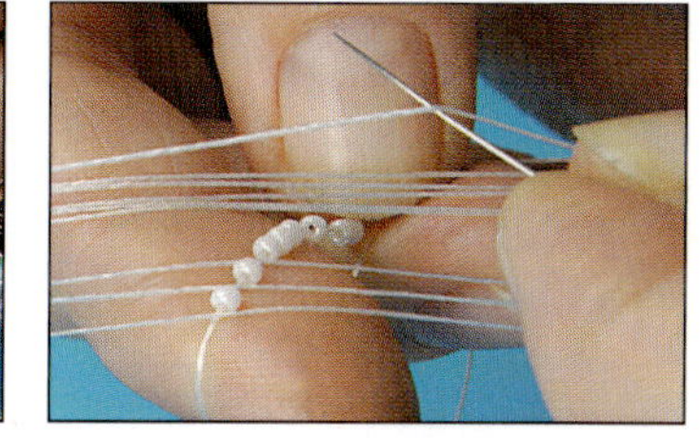

4. Move warp threads into place with the needle. There should be a bead (total of 8 beads) between each thread (total of 9 threads).

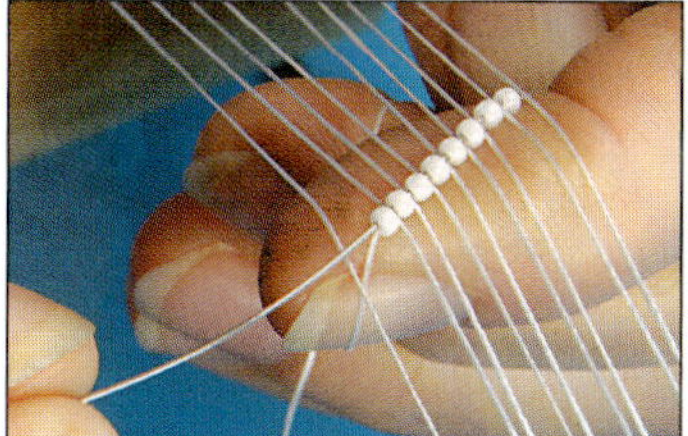

5. Push up on the beads. Pass the needle into all beads going OVER the warp threads. This process will secure beads on each row.

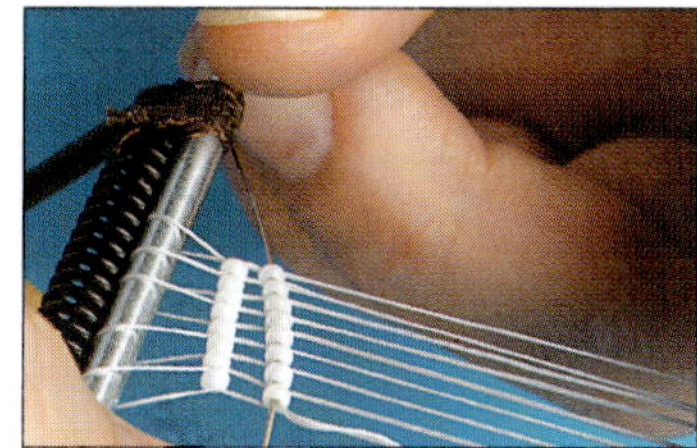

6. To check that the needle has not gone thru any of the warp threads, move beads up and down a little, they should move freely.

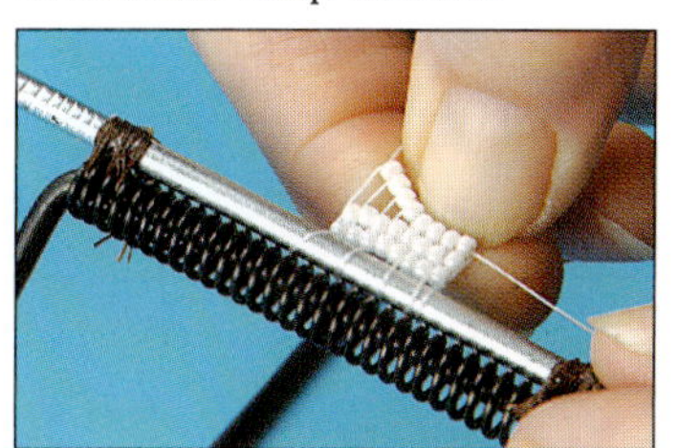

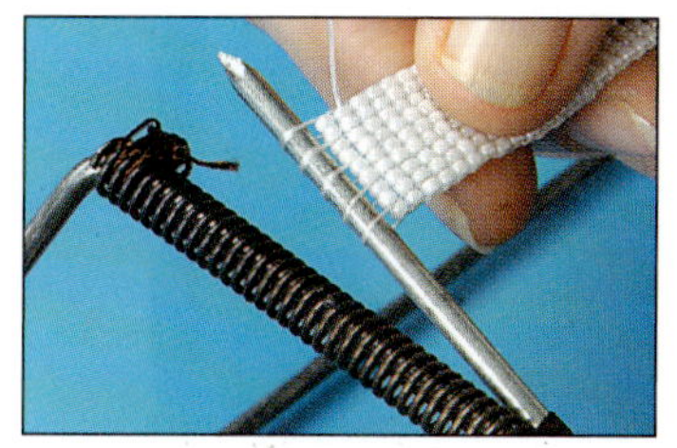

7. Add the 2nd and 3rd rows. Beading will be much easier now with the warp thread held in position by the first row. Push the row of beads toward the end of the loom. Weave bracelet very tightly.

8. When the bracelet is complete, remove it from the loom.

9. Push beads toward the ends to fill the empty warp threads.

10. Continue to push beads to the end to fill empty threads.

Ball Closure - Use an E-bead the same color as seed beads. Follow the diagram to begin.

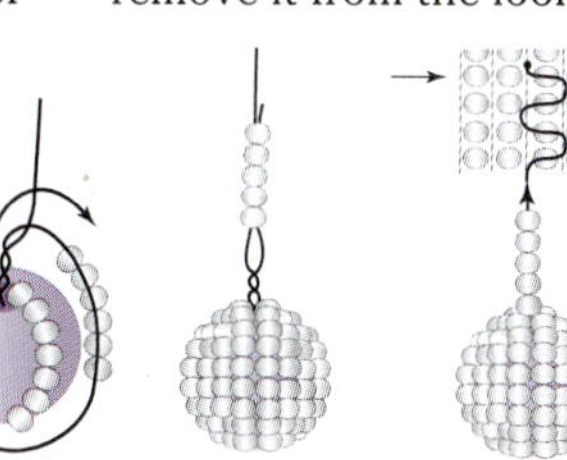

Continue wrapping seed beads around E-bead, knotting and pulling taut until bead is covered.

To Finish - Weave the ends of thread back thru some beads, tie off with a knot, weave thru more threads to hide the end.

Helpful Hints

Start adding rows of beads at one end of the loom. Continue adding rows in the desired pattern until you reach the other end.

Tip: Beads vary in size so you may need to delete or add a few rows of beads in the pattern to make the right length of bracelet.

Tip: Most bracelets are woven to be 6" long. Use multiple loops on the Loop Closure to adjust the final bracelet to fit your wrist.

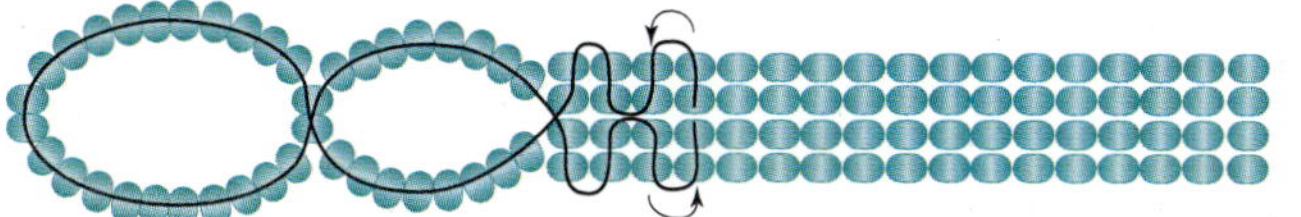

Loop Closure - On the other end of bracelet, add new thread then make a double loop (be sure loops are large enough to go over the ball).

Beginner Bracelets ... Only 8 Beads Wide

Blue Diagonal - Beads (Black, Blue Iridescent, Royal Blue Silver Lined, Clear Aqua Lined, Lavender Pearl)
Prepare loom with 9 strands of Black thread (8 beads).

Blue Rectangle - Beads (Royal Blue Silver Lined, Dark Blue Iridescent, Lavender Pearl) **Prepare loom** with 9 strands of Blue thread (8 beads).

Xs on Blue - Beads (Gold Silver Lined, Royal Blue Silver Lined, Lavender Pearl, Brown Transparent)
Prepare loom with 9 strands of Black thread (8 beads).

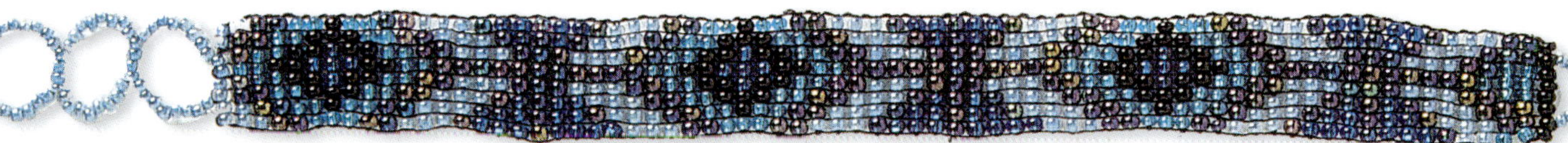

Diamonds on Blue - Beads (Aqua Silver Lined, Black, Royal Blue Silver Lined, Clear Aqua Lined, Purple Iridescent)
Prepare loom with 9 strands of Black thread (8 beads).

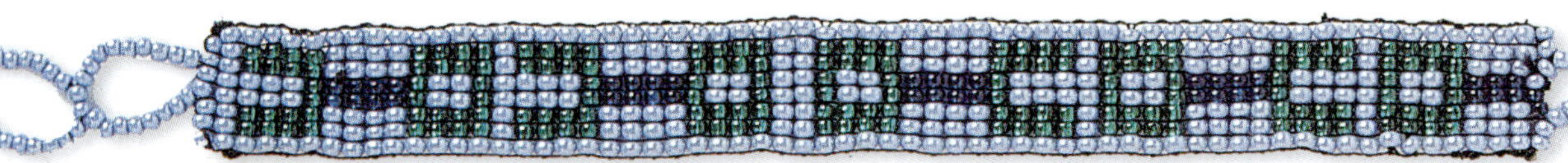

Geometrics on Lavender - Beads (Lavender Pearl, Green Transparent, Royal Blue Transparent)
Prepare loom with 9 strands of Black thread (8 beads).

Blue Trees - Beads (Black, Lavender Pearl, Royal Blue Silver Lined) **Prepare loom** with 9 strands of Black thread (8 beads).

Squares & Diamonds - Beads (Gold Silver Lined, Green Iridescent, Lavender Pearl, Royal Blue Transparent, Black)
Prepare loom with 9 strands of Black thread (8 beads).

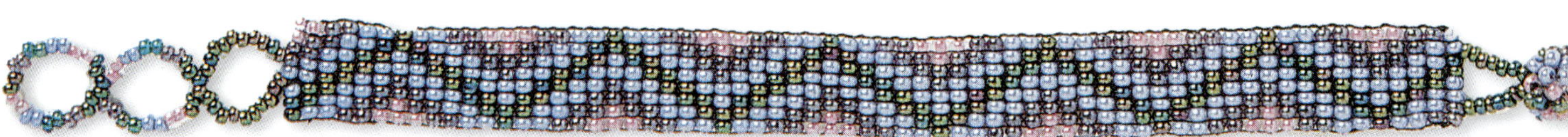

Zig Zags - Beads (Hot Pink Lined, Clear Mauve Lined, Lavender Pearl, Green Iridescent) **Prepare loom** with 9 strands of Black thread (8 beads).

Diamonds - Beads (Royal Blue Transparent, Lavender Pearl, Clear Pink Lined, Green Transparent)
Prepare loom with 9 strands of Black thread (8 beads).

How to Make a Loom for Bracelets

This loom is just the right length for bracelets so you don't have to weave the end threads back into the beads.

With just a scrap piece of wood, 6 large 3½" nails and/or wire rods (strong coat hanger wire works great), you can make your own loom... an easy loom that is the perfect length for you to weave bracelets.

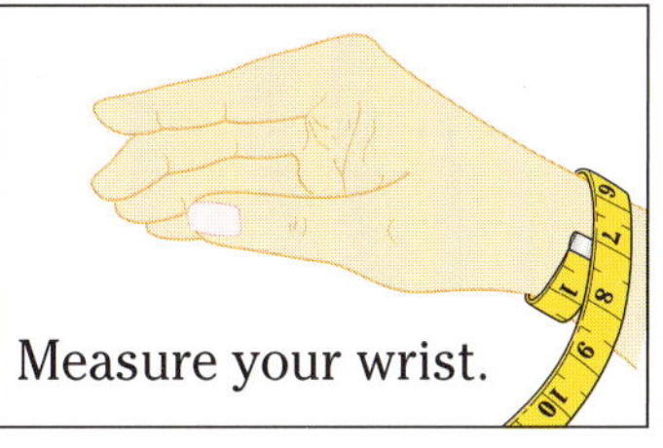

1. A 6" long bracelet (including ball & loop) will fit wrist sizes 5" to 7" around.

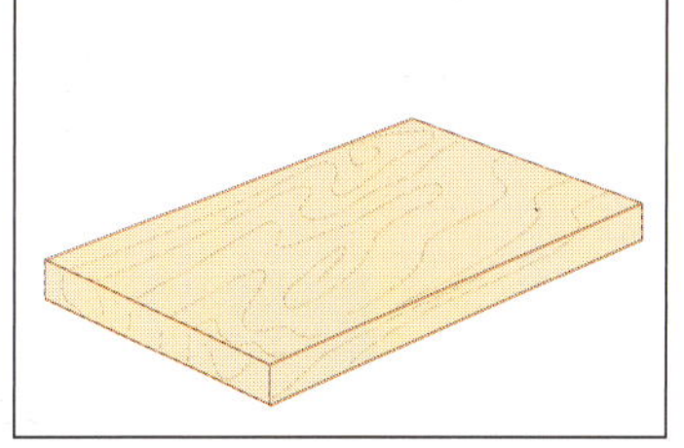

2. Use a piece of wood 1" thick x 6" x 10" for the base.

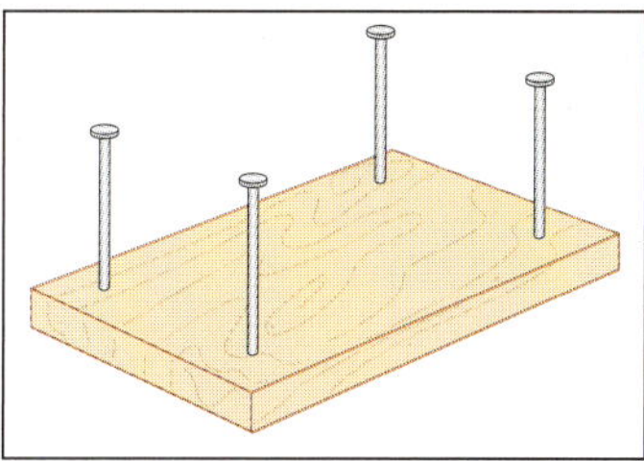

3. Hammer 4 long nails in the wood (3" x 6¼" apart).

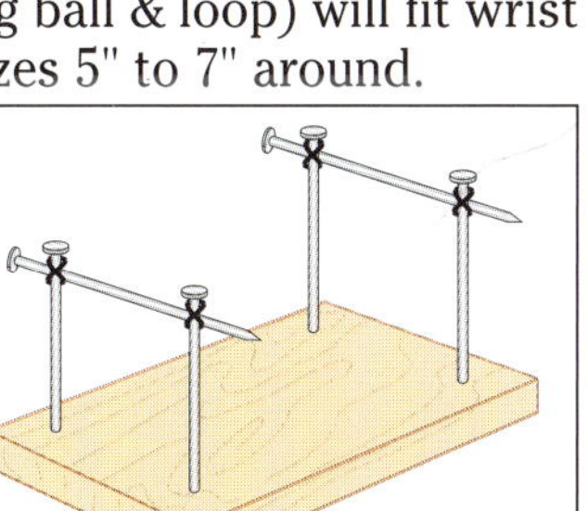

4. Tie a 4" length of metal rod (a nail or coat hanger wire) across each end.

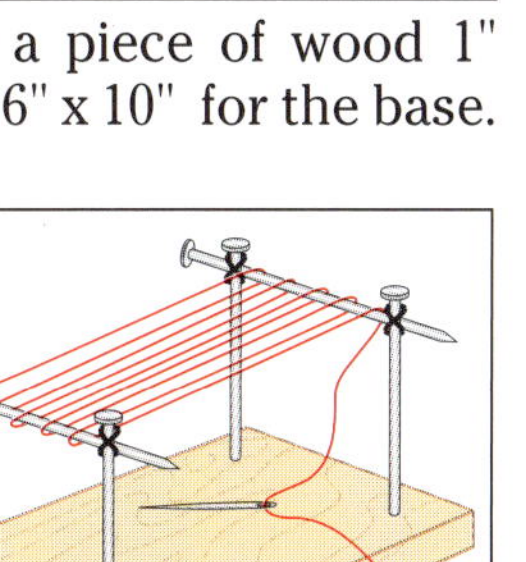

5. Tie thread securely to the metal rod. Leave 12" tail of thread. Wrap thread around rods. Count warp threads according to instructions for each bracelet.

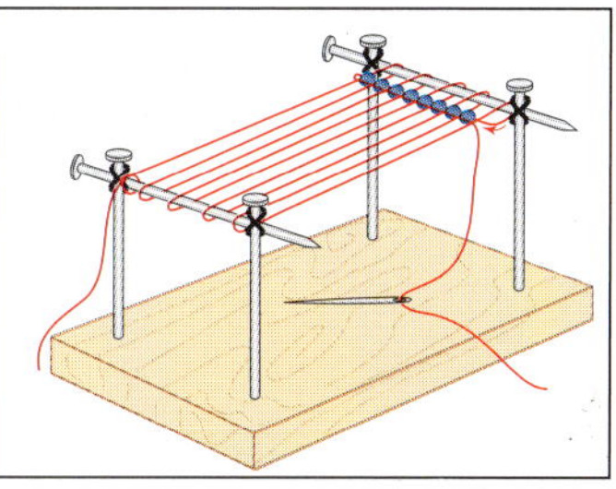

6. Begin beading first row.

Diamonds on Gold - Beads (Dark Gold Silver Lined, Clear Silver Lined, Orange Transparent) **Prepare loom** with 9 strands of Brown thread (8 beads).

Birds - Beads (Dark Red Transparent, Royal Blue Silver Lined, Gold Silver Lined, Clear Yellow Lined) **Prepare loom** with 9 strands of Black thread (8 beads).

Easy to Make Beginner Bracelets Only 8 beads wide!

Crosses - Beads (Clear Green Iridescent, Lavender Pearl, Purple Iridescent) **Prepare loom** with 9 strands of Black thread (8 beads).

Girls - Beads (Peach Pearl, Blue Pearl, Dark Red Transparent, Gold Silver Lined, Clear Green Lined, Black) **Prepare loom** with 9 strands of Black thread (8 beads).

Diamonds - Beads (Black, Royal Blue Silver Lined, Gold Silver Lined, Clear Silver Lined) **Prepare loom** with 8 strands of Black thread (7 beads).

Black & Red - Beads (Black, Red, Lavender Pearl) **Prepare loom** with 9 strands of Black thread (8 beads).

Multi Diamonds - Beads (Black, Yellow Green Lined, Blue Iridescent, Clear Silver Lined, Red Silver Lined) **Prepare loom** with 9 strands of Black thread (8 beads).

Entwined - Beads (Black, Hot Pink Pearl, White Pearl) **Prepare loom** with 9 strands of Black thread (8 beads).

Great Patterns for Fun & Easy Bracelets for Beginners... Only 8 Beads Wide

Gold Zig Zag - Beads (Black, Dark Red Transparent, Gold Transparent, Gold Silver Lined) **Prepare loom** with 9 strands of Black thread (8 beads).

Red Breasted Bird - Beads (Clear Silver Lined, Green Transparent, Clear White Lined, Aqua Transparent, Red Transparent, Black, Light Blue Transparent) **Prepare loom** with 9 strands of Gray thread (8 beads).

Fish - Transparent Beads (Green, Orange, Royal Blue) **Prepare loom** with 9 strands of Gray thread (8 beads).

Black & Lime - Beads (Black, Lime Green Transparent, Clear Gold Silver Lined) **Prepare loom** with 9 strands of Black thread (8 beads).

Black Geometric - Beads (Black, Green Transparent, Gold Transparent, Clear Pink Lined) **Prepare loom** with 9 strands of Black thread (8 beads).

Stairstep - Beads (Black, Green Transparent, Clear Lime Green Lined, Purple Iridescent) **Prepare loom** with 9 strands of Black thread (8 beads).

Beginner Bracelets ... Only 8 Beads Wide

Gold & Silver Spiral - Beads (Black, Clear Gold Silver Lined, Clear Silver Lined) **Prepare loom** with 9 strands of Black thread (8 beads).

Swirls - Beads (Black, Clear Gold Silver Lined) **Prepare loom** with 8 strands of Black thread (7 beads).

Black & Silver Diamonds - Beads (Black, Clear Silver Lined) **Prepare loom** with 9 strands of Black thread (8 beads).

Squares - Beads (Black, Clear White Lined, Gunmetal, Gold Silver Lined) **Prepare loom** with 9 strands of Black thread (8 beads).

Grape & Gold - Beads (Clear Blue Iridescent, Mauve Transparent, Gold Transparent, Black) **Prepare loom** with 9 strands of Black thread (8 beads).

Trees - Beads (Black, Gunmetal, Gold Transparent) **Prepare loom** with 9 strands of Black thread (8 beads).

Girl - Beads (Black, Red Iridescent, Clear Silver Lined, Clear Pink Lined, Gunmetal, Clear Green Lined, Clear Gold Silver Lined, Clear Pink Silver Lined, Aqua Transparent) **Prepare loom** with 9 strands of Black thread (8 beads).

Chevrons - Beads (Black, Teal Transparent, Brown Transparent, Clear Gold Silver Lined, Clear Silver Lined) **Prepare loom** with 9 strands of Black thread (8 beads).

Geometric - Beads (Black, Clear Silver Lined, Green Iridescent, Pink Transparent) **Prepare loom** with 9 strands of Black thread (8 beads).

Building Blocks - Beads (Green Iridescent, Clear Pink Lined) **Prepare loom** with 17 strands of Black thread (16 beads).

Waves 1 - Beads (Black, Gunmetal, Clear Silver Lined) **Prepare loom** with 17 strands of Black thread (16 beads).

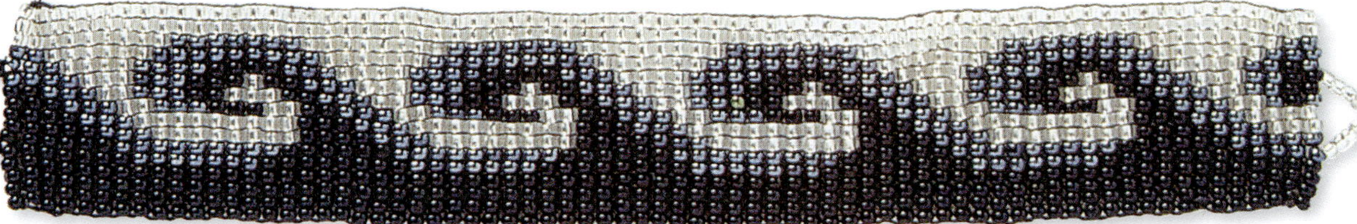

Waves 2 - Beads (Black, Gunmetal, Clear Silver Lined) **Prepare loom** with 17 strands of Black thread (16 beads).

Paving Stones - Beads (Black, Gunmetal, Clear Silver Lined) **Prepare loom** with 17 strands of Black thread (16 beads).

Beautiful Bracelets ... 16 Beads Wide

Arrows - Beads (Clear Silver Lined, Dark Gold Transparent, Clear Gold Silver Lined, Teal Transparent) **Prepare loom** with 17 strands of White thread (16 beads).

Large Diamonds - Beads (Lime Green Transparent, Teal Transparent, Green Transparent, Dark Gold Transparent, Clear Silver Lined, Clear Gold Silver Lined) **Prepare loom** with 17 strands of White thread (16 beads).

Large Chevrons - Beads (Dark Gold Transparent, Clear Gold Silver Lined, Clear Silver Lined, Teal Silver Lined, Green Transparent, Dark Green Iridescent) **Prepare loom** with 17 strands of Black thread (16 beads).

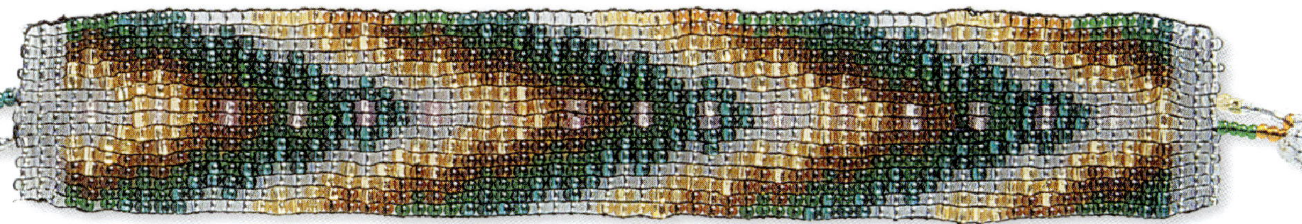

Long Chevrons - Beads (Dark Gold Transparent, Clear Gold Silver Lined, Teal Silver Lined, Green Transparent, Pink Iridescent, Clear Pink Lined) **Prepare loom** with 17 strands of Black thread (16 beads).

Pyramids - Beads (Lime Green Pearl, Dark Green, Teal Transparent, Aqua Silver Lined, Lime Green Silver Lined) **Prepare loom** with 17 strands of Black thread (16 beads).

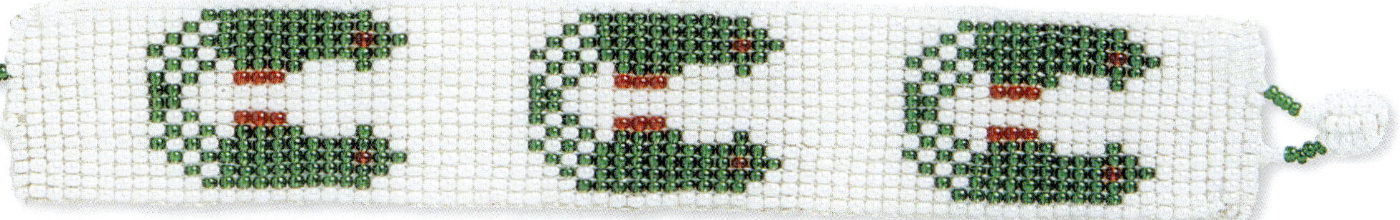

Facing Birds - Beads (White Pearl, Green Silver Lined, Red Transparent) **Prepare loom** with 17 strands of White thread (16 beads).

Diamond Links - Beads (Blue Iridescent, Clear Orange Iridescent, Clear Yellow Lined, Green Transparent, Red Transparent) **Prepare loom** with 17 strands of Black thread (16 beads).

Bracelets ... 15 to 24 Beads Wide

Large X's & O's - Beads (Royal Blue Transparent, Clear Gold Silver Lined, Green Transparent, Clear Silver Lined, Clear Dark Gold Silver Lined, Lavender Pearl) **Prepare loom** with 17 strands of Blue thread (16 beads).

X's & O's - Beads (Dark Gold Transparent, Gunmetal, Clear Silver Lined, Clear Gold Silver Lined, Teal Silver Lined) **Prepare loom** with 17 strands of Black thread (16 beads).

Zigs & Zags - Beads (Black, Aqua Transparent, Purple Iridescent, Clear Blue Iridescent, Clear Orange Iridescent) **Prepare loom** with 17 strands of Black thread (16 beads).

Lightning - Beads (Black, Dark Gold Transparent, Purple Iridescent, Blue Iridescent, Lime Green Pearl, Clear Aqua Silver Lined) **Prepare loom** with 17 strands of Black thread (16 beads).

Diamonds - Beads (Black, Clear Blue Iridescent, Royal Blue Iridescent, Green Transparent) **Prepare loom** with 16 strands of Black thread (15 beads).

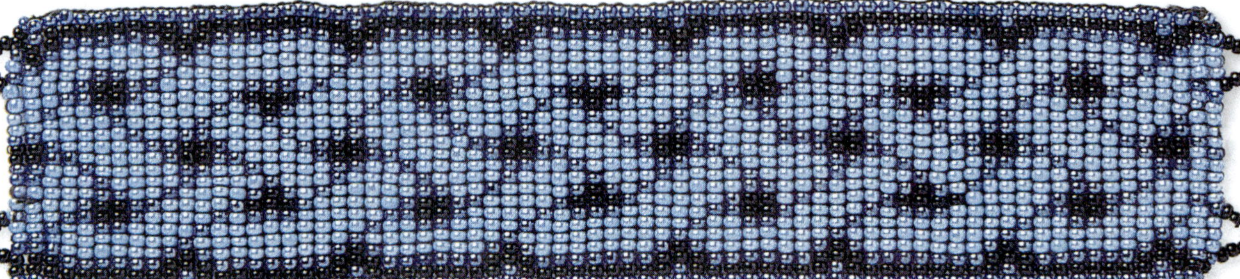

Blue Celtic Knots - Beads (Clear Blue Iridescent, Black, Lavender Pearl) **Prepare loom** with 25 strands of Black thread (24 beads).

Waves - Beads (Black, Royal Blue Silver Lined, Aqua Silver Lined) **Prepare loom** with 17 strands of Black thread (16 beads).

Bracelets ... 15 to 24 Beads Wide

Butterflies - Beads (Blue Silver Lined, Clear Silver Lined, Green Silver Lined, Clear Yellow Lined, Red Transparent) **Prepare loom** with 17 strands of Blue thread (16 beads).

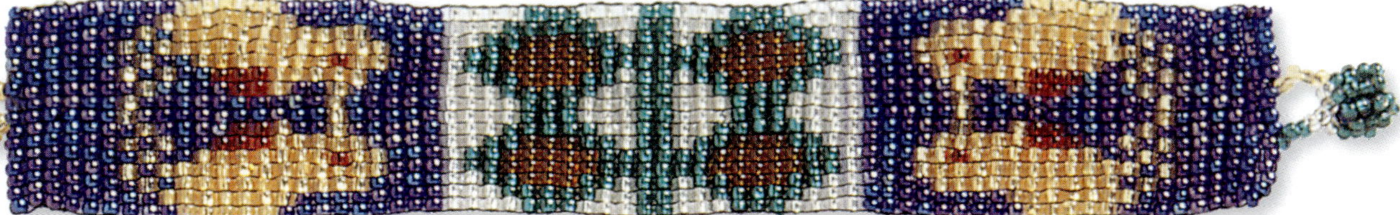

Love Birds - Beads (Purple Iridescent, Clear Gold Silver Lined, Red Transparent, Clear Silver Lined, Teal Transparent, Dark Gold Transparent) **Prepare loom** with 17 strands of Black thread (16 beads).

Rainbow - Beads (Royal Blue Silver Lined, Clear Dark Gold Silver Lined, Clear Silver Lined, Clear Gold Silver Lined, Clear Pink Silver Lined, Green Silver Lined, Purple Iridescent, Black, Lavender Pearl) **Prepare loom** with 17 strands of Blue thread (16 beads).

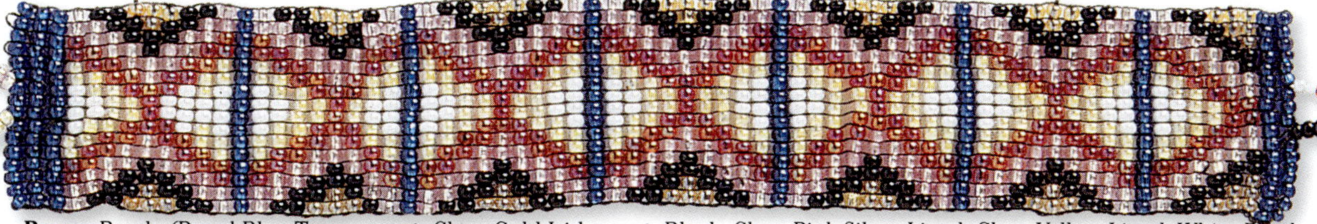

Bows - Beads (Royal Blue Transparent, Clear Gold Iridescent, Black, Clear Pink Silver Lined, Clear Yellow Lined, White Pearl, Red Iridescent) **Prepare loom** with 17 strands of Black thread (16 beads).

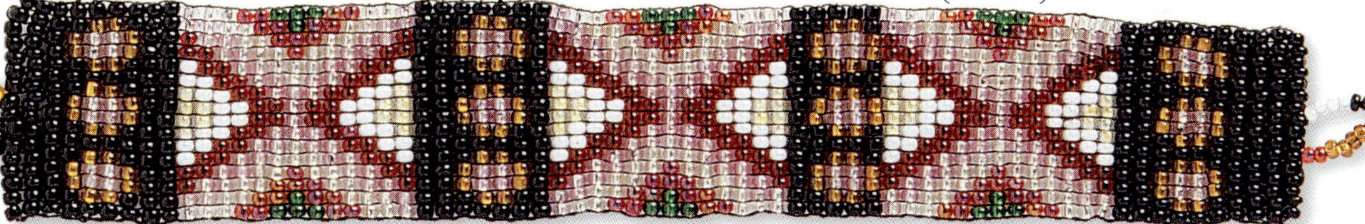

Large Bows - Beads (Black, Clear Gold Silver Lined, Clear Pink Silver Lined, Green Silver Lined, Red Iridescent, Clear Silver Lined, Red Transparent, White Pearl, Clear Yellow Lined) **Prepare loom** with 17 strands of Black thread (16 beads).

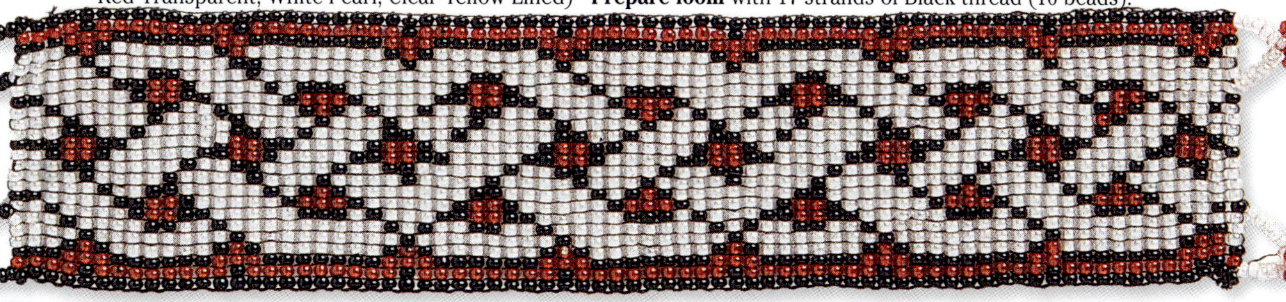

White Celtic Knots - Beads (Black, Red Silver Lined, Clear White Lined) **Prepare loom** with 25 strands of Black thread (24 beads).

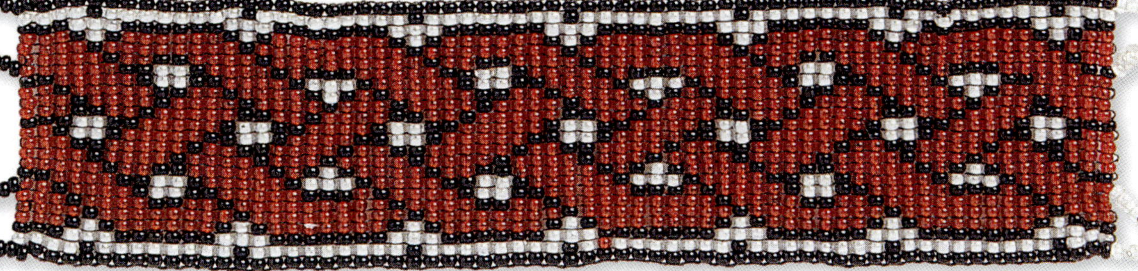

Red Celtic Knots - Beads (Black, Red Transparent, Clear White Lined) **Prepare loom** with 25 strands of Black thread (24 beads).

Primary Diamonds - Beads (Teal Silver Lined, Clear Silver Lined, Red Silver Lined, Royal Blue Silver Lined
Prepare loom with 31 strands of Black thread (30 beads).

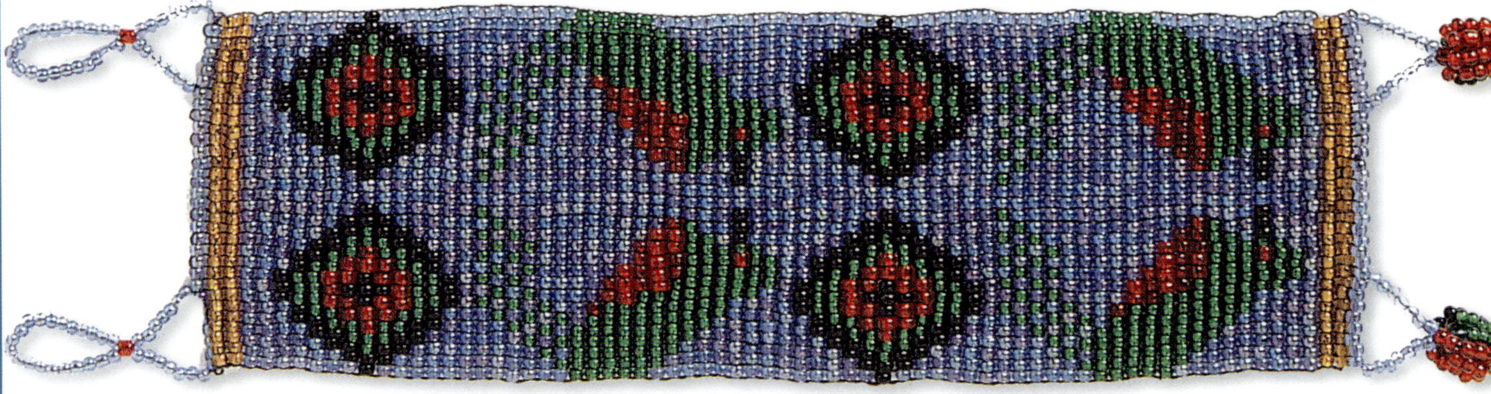

Parrots - Beads (Blue Iridescent, Brown Transparent, Green Silver Lined, Red Silver Lined
Prepare loom with 33 strands of Blue thread (32 beads).

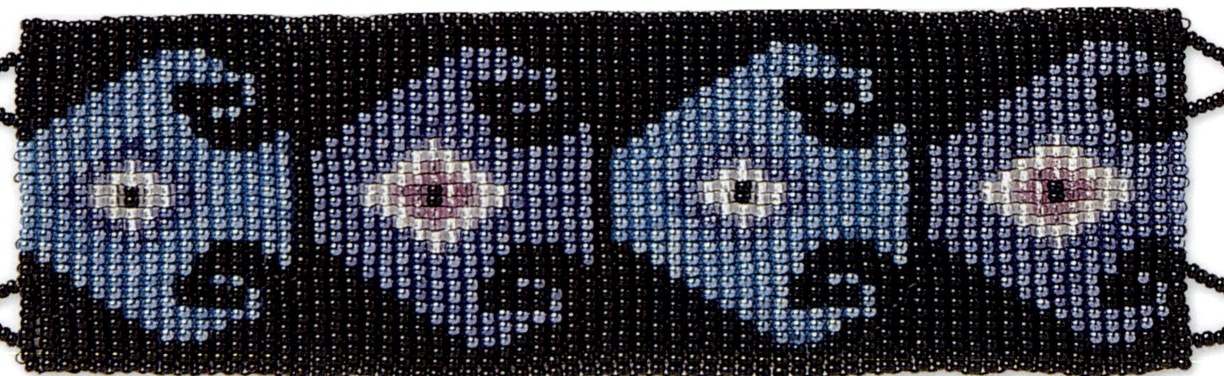

Urns - Beads (Black, Clear Blue Iridescent, Clear Silver Lined, Pink Silver Lined, Aqua Silver Lined)
Prepare loom with 33 strands of Black thread (32 beads).

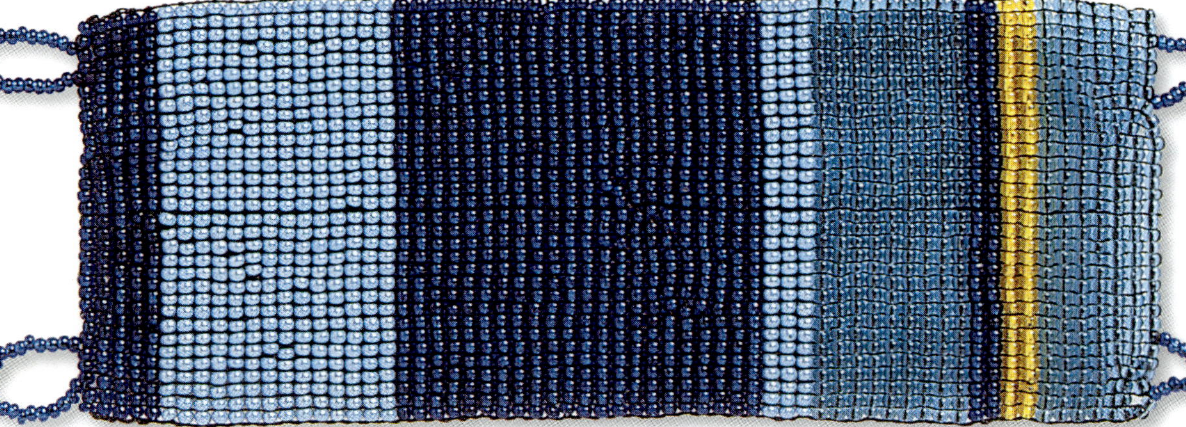

Striped Blanket - Beads (Royal Blue Transparent, Blue Pearl, Teal Transparent, Clear Yellow Silver Lined)
Prepare loom with 33 strands of Black thread (32 beads).

Fancy Bracelets ... 32 Beads Wide

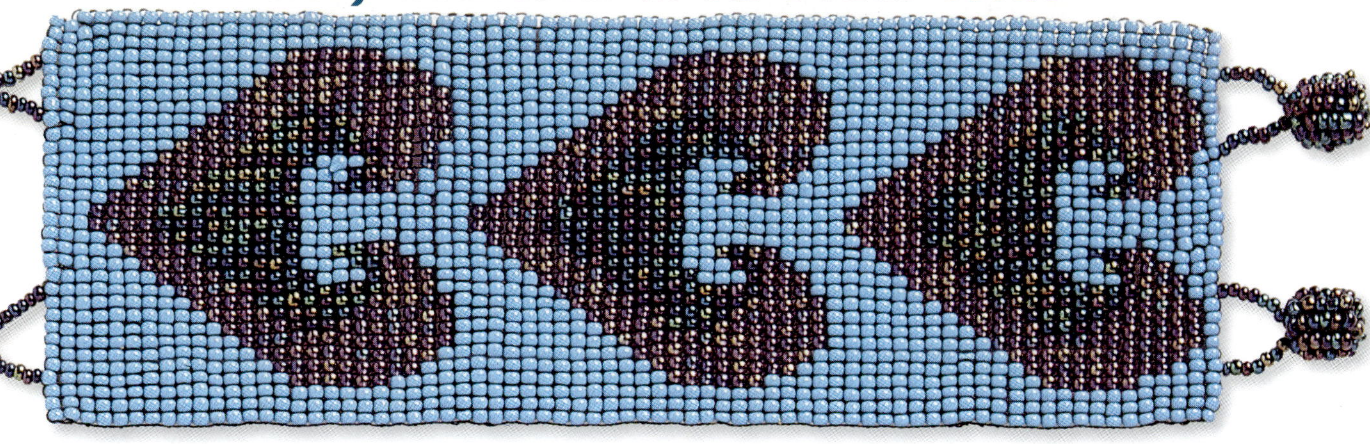

Open Hearts - Beads (Clear Mauve Iridescent, Black Iridescent, Sky Blue) **Prepare loom** with 33 strands of Black thread (32 beads).

Patchwork - Beads (Clear Pink Lined, Black, Teal Pearl, Blue Pearl, Royal Blue Silver Lined) **Prepare loom** with 33 strands of Black thread (32 beads).

Indian Blanket - Beads (Clear Gold Silver Lined, Black, Clear Red Iridescent, Sky Blue) **Prepare loom** with 33 strands of Black thread (32 beads).

Stained Glass - Beads (Gunmetal, Turquoise, Lavender Pearl, Black), Silver Lined (Lime Green, Mauve, Gold, Red, Yellow), Clear Lined (Pink, Hot Pink, Silver), Iridescent (Purple, Orange, Clear Gold) **Prepare loom** with 33 strands of Black thread (32 beads).

Triangle Butterflies - Beads (Black, White Pearl, Royal Blue, Clear Red Iridescent, Green Pearl, Red Iridescent, Green Transparent, Turquoise Silver Lined, Mauve Transparent, Orange Silver Lined) **Prepare loom** with 33 strands of Black thread (32 beads).

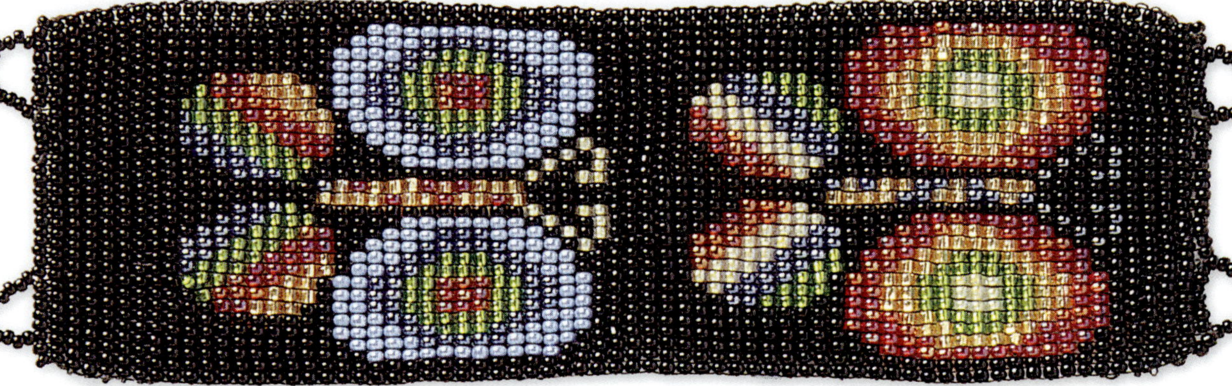

Butterflies - Beads (Black, Blue Iridescent, Lime Green Silver Lined, Clear Red Iridescent, Clear Gold Silver Lined, Lavender Pearl, Clear Yellow Lined) **Prepare loom** with 33 strands of Black thread (32 beads).

Geometric Butterflies- Beads (Black, Clear Gold Silver Lined, Royal Blue Transparent, Lavender Pearl, Orange, Green Transparent, Yellow Silver Lined) **Prepare loom** with 33 strands of Black thread (32 beads).

Flower Bracelet ... 31 Beads Wide

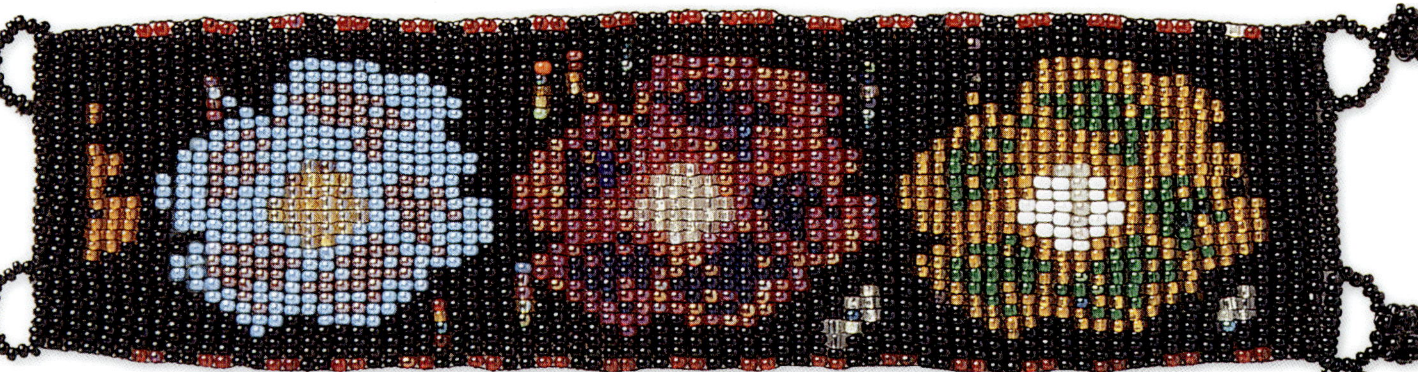

Flowers - Beads (Black, Orange Silver Lined, Aqua Transparent, Aqua Pearl, Red Iridescent, Gold Silver Lined, Clear Red Iridescent, Royal Blue Transparent, Clear Silver Lined, Green Silver Lined, White, White Pearl) **Prepare loom** with 32 strands of Black thread (31 beads).

Fancy Bracelets ... 32 Beads Wide

Eagle - Beads (Royal Blue Silver Lined, Clear Gold Iridescent, Black, White) **Prepare loom** with 33 strands of Blue thread (32 beads).

Zigs & Zags - Beads (Black, Royal Blue Silver Lined, Aqua Transparent, Clear Silver Lined, Clear Mauve Iridescent)
Prepare loom with 33 strands of Black thread (32 beads).

Art Deco - Beads (Black, Clear Green Lined, Gold Silver Lined, Clear Aqua Lined, Green Iridescent)
Prepare loom with 33 strands of Black thread (32 beads).

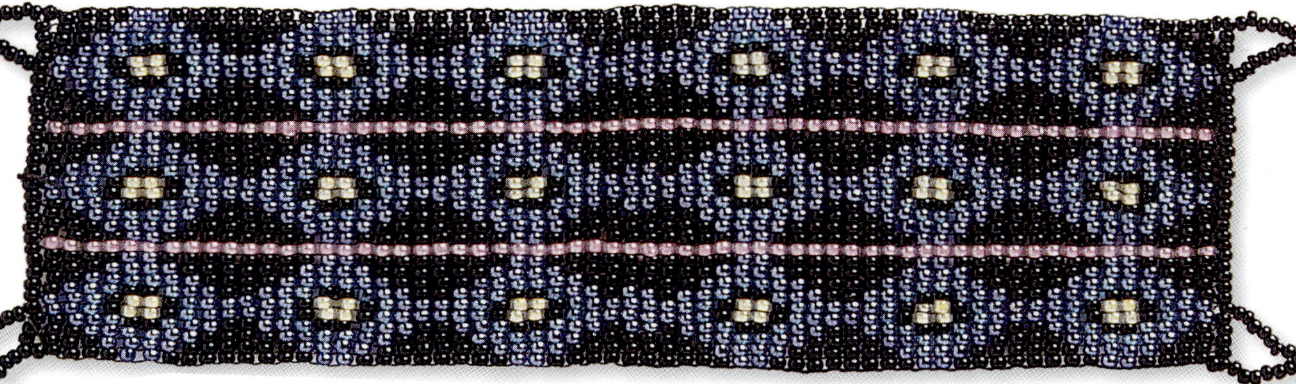

Diamond Rows - Beads (Black, Clear Blue Iridescent, Aqua Silver Lined, Clear Yellow Lined, Clear Pink Lined)
Prepare loom with 33 strands of Black thread (32 beads).

Golden Bracelets ... 32 Beads Wide

Golden Waves - Beads (Clear Dark Gold Silver Lined, Black, Clear Gold Silver Lined, Green Transparent, Blue Transparent)
Prepare loom with 33 strands of Black thread (32 beads).

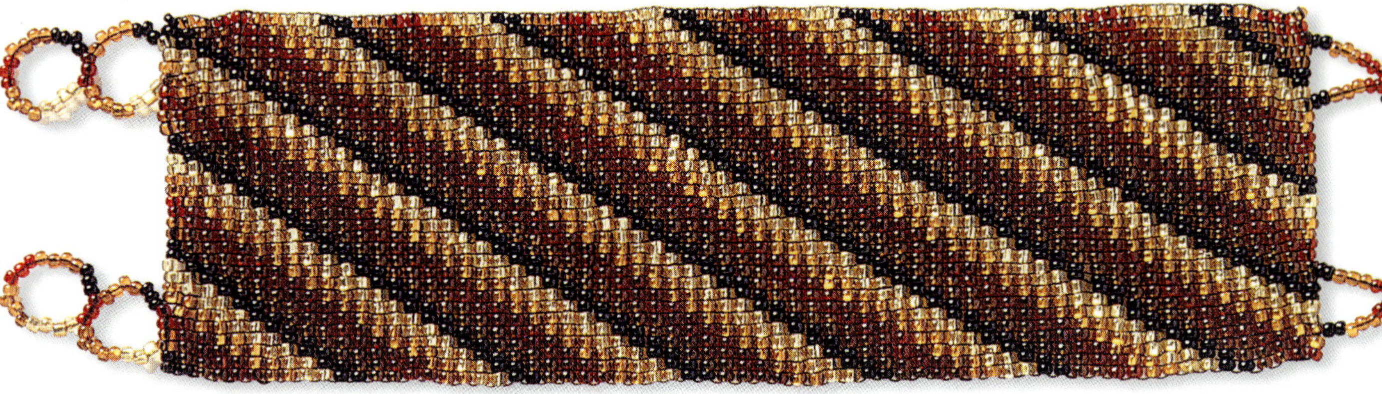

Diagonals - Beads (Black, Dark Gold Silver Lined, Brown Transparent, Red Transparent, Clear Gold Silver Lined)
Prepare loom with 33 strands of Black thread (32 beads).

Interlocked Diamonds - Beads (Clear Dark Gold Silver Lined, Clear Silver Lined, Black)
Prepare loom with 33 strands of Tan thread (32 beads).

Greek Key - Beads (Black, Gold Transparent) **Prepare loom** with 33 strands of Black thread (32 beads).

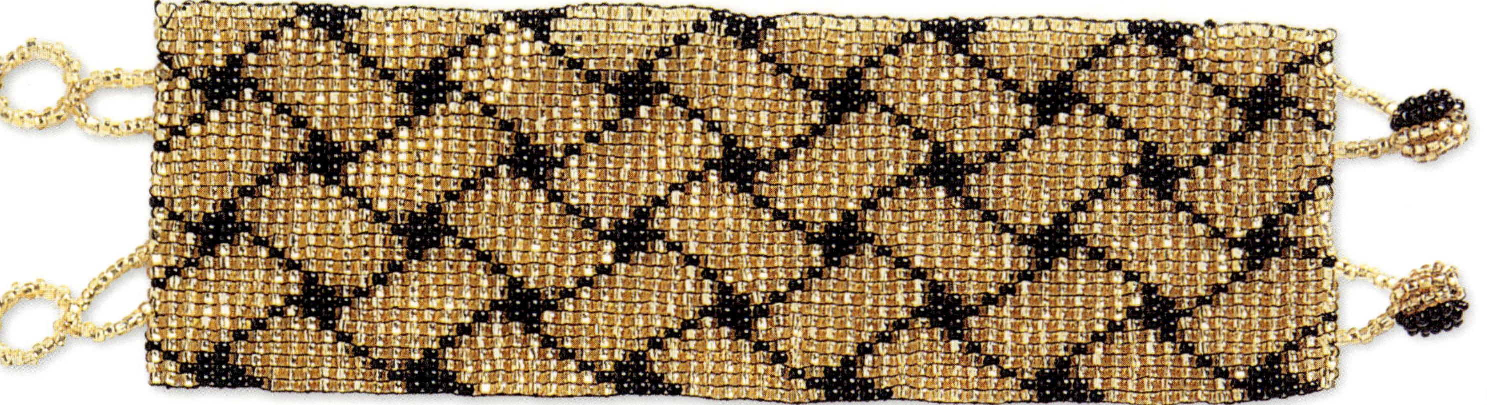

Gold & Black Weave - Beads (Black, Clear Gold Silver Lined) **Prepare loom** with 33 strands of Black thread (32 beads).

Gold & Black Stripes - Beads (Black, Clear Gold Silver Lined) **Prepare loom** with 33 strands of Black thread (32 beads).

Gold & Black Zig Zags - Beads (Black, Clear Gold Silver Lined) **Prepare loom** with 33 strands of Black thread (32 beads).

Golden Bracelets ... 32 Beads Wide

Golden Blanket - Beads (Black, Clear Gold Silver Lined, Brown Transparent, Clear Silver Lined)
Prepare loom with 33 strands of Black thread (32 beads).

Cow - Beads (Black, White) **Prepare loom** with 9 strands of Black thread (8 beads).

Zebra - Beads (Black, White Pearl) **Prepare loom** with 9 strands of White thread (8 beads).

Tiger Cub - Beads (Black, Clear Gold Silver Lined) **Prepare loom** with 9 strands of Gold thread (8 beads).

Safari Bracelets ... 8 to 32 Beads Wide

Giraffe - Beads (Clear Yellow Lined, Clear Dark Gold Silver Lined) **Prepare loom** with 33 strands of Yellow thread (32 beads).

Leopard - Beads (Black, Clear Gold Silver Lined, Brown Silver Lined) **Prepare loom** with 33 strands of Yellow thread (32 beads).

Tiger - Beads (Black, Clear Gold Silver Lined) **Prepare loom** with 33 strands of Black thread (32 beads).

Small Giraffe - Beads (Clear Yellow Lined, Dark Clear Gold Silver Lined) **Prepare loom** with 9 strands of Gold thread (8 beads).

Jaguar - Beads (Black, Clear Gold Silver Lined, Clear Gold Iridescent, Mauve Iridescent) **Prepare loom** with 33 strands of Black thread (32 beads).

Be Creative!

Make a Small Bag from any wide bracelet pattern in this book.

Safari Amulet Bag

SIZE: 3¾" x 2"

First make a bracelet size piece with the spotted Leopard design.

Leopard - Beads (Black, Clear Gold Silver Lined, Brown Transparent)

Prepare loom with 43 strands of Tan thread (42 beads).

INSTRUCTIONS: Make the beaded pattern 9¼" long. Fold up 3¾" and sew the sides together matching the rows of beads. Fold the remaining flap down. Make a ball button and a beaded loop closure.

STRAP - Make the desired length of daisy chain following diagrams below.

Tiger, Tiger - Beads (Dark Green, Rust, Black, White, Cream Pearl, Clear Gold Iridescent, Clear Clear Gold Silver Lined)
Prepare loom with 33 strands of Black thread (32 beads).

Beautiful Bracelets ... 32 Beads Wide

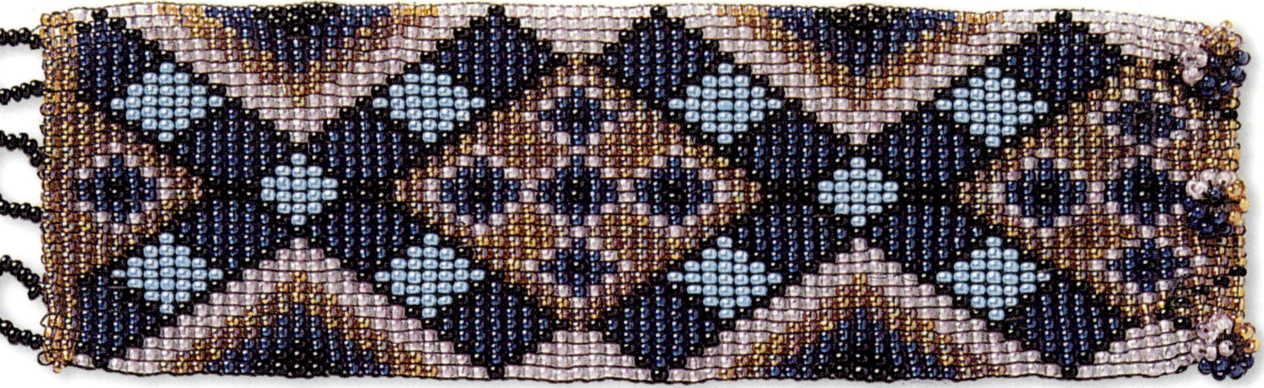

Native Rug - Beads (Black, Clear Orange Iridescent, Royal Blue Silver Lined, Aqua Pearl, Clear Pink Lined)
Prepare loom with 33 strands of Black thread (32 beads).

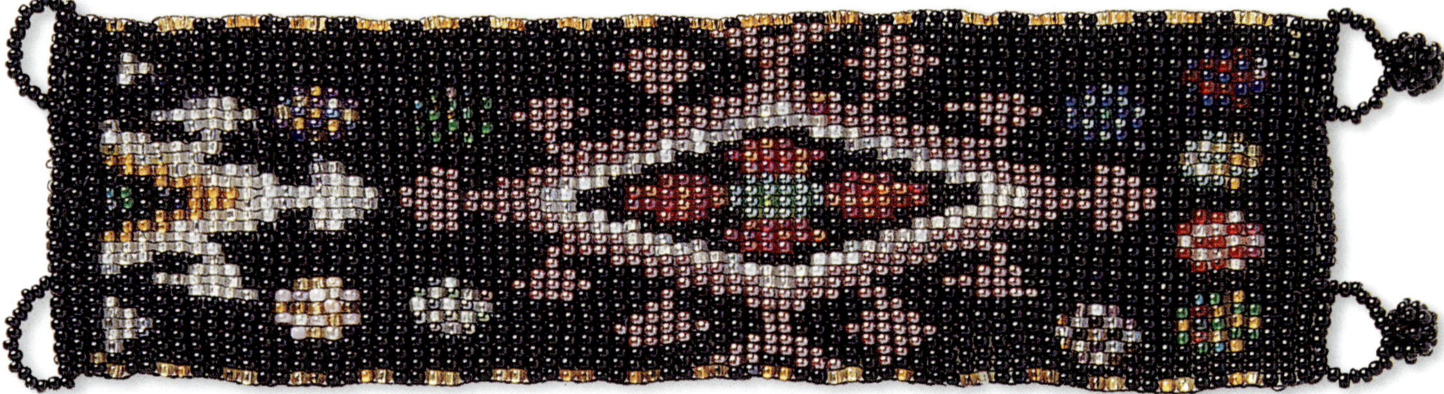

Black Rug - Beads (Black, Clear Silver Lined, Clear Gold Silver Lined, Green Silver Lined, Royal Blue Silver Lined, Dark Pink Pearl, Clear Red Iridescent, Clear Green Iridescent, Brown Transparent) **Prepare loom** with 33 strands of Black thread (32 beads).

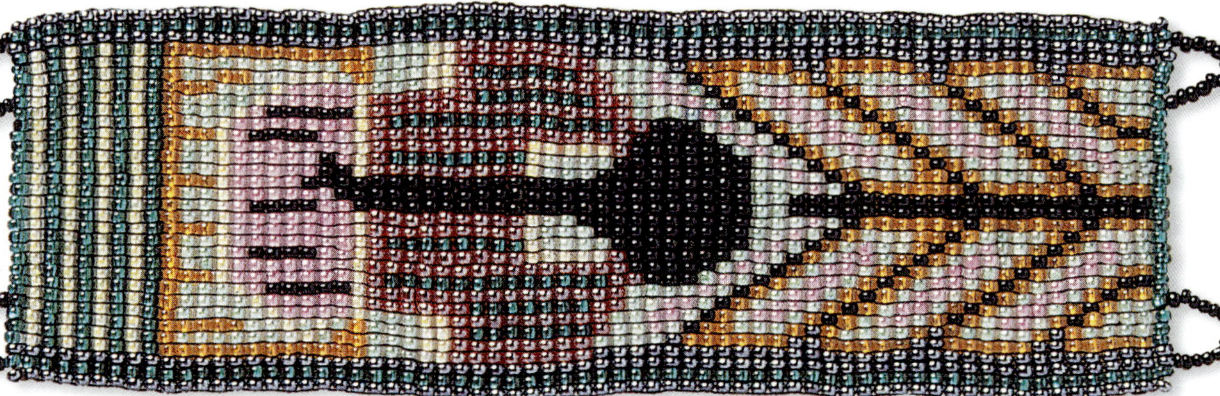

Rug Weaver - Beads (Black, Gunmetal, Green Silver Lined, Orange Silver Lined, Clear Green Lined, Clear Pink Lined, Clear Red Iridescent, Clear Yellow Lined) **Prepare loom** with 33 strands of Black thread (32 beads).

Pink Flowers - Beads (Black, Clear Gold Silver Lined, Green Silver Lined, Clear Pink Lined, Clear Hot Pink Lined)
Prepare loom with 33 strands of Black thread (32 beads).

Arrowheads - Beads (Black, Green Iridescent, Clear Mauve Silver Lined, Clear Pink Lined, Clear Gold Silver Lined)
Prepare loom with 33 strands of Black thread (32 beads).

Mask - Beads (Black, Gold Iridescent, Green Silver Lined, Clear Peach Lined, Gunmetal, Clear Pink Lined)
Prepare loom with 33 strands of Black thread (32 beads).

Double Waves - Beads (Black, Clear Peach Lined, Royal Blue Iridescent, Clear Aqua Lined) **Prepare loom** with 33 strands of Black thread (32 beads).

Beautiful Bracelets ... 32 Beads Wide

Spiders, Symbol of Mother Earth - Beads (Mauve Silver Lined, Orange Silver Lined, Gray Silver Lined, White, Black)
Prepare loom with 33 strands of Black thread (32 beads).

Elegant Bracelets ... 32 Beads Wide

Interlocking Diamonds - Beads (Black, Clear Gold Silver Lined, Purple Iridescent) Prepare loom with 33 strands of Black thread (32 beads).

Double Zig Zag - Beads (Black, Clear Silver Lined, Clear Gold Silver Lined) **Prepare loom** with 33 strands of Black thread (32 beads).

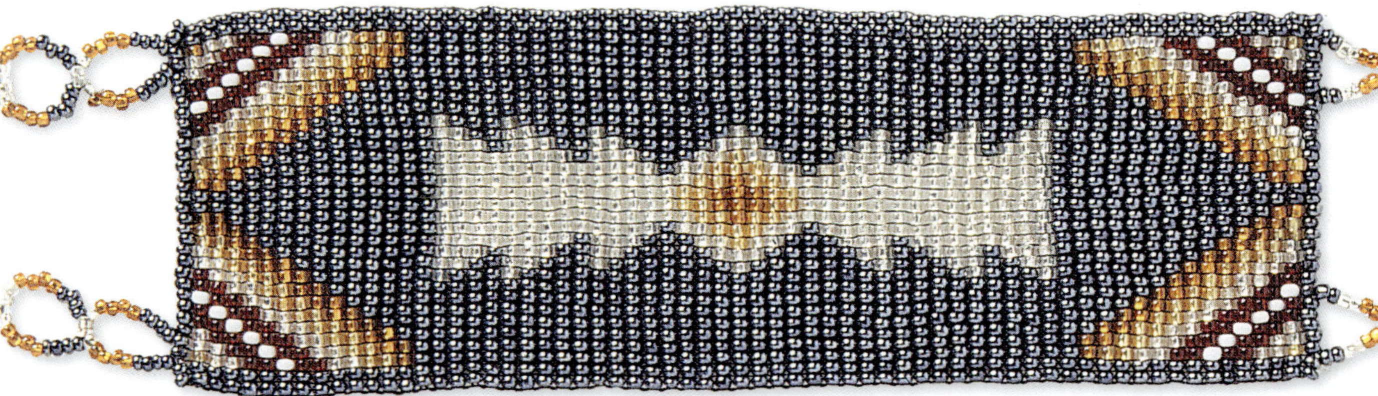

Single Motif - Beads (Gunmetal, Clear Gold Silver Lined, Clear Silver Lined, Red Transparent, White, Dark Clear Gold Silver Lined)
Prepare loom with 33 strands of Black thread (32 beads).

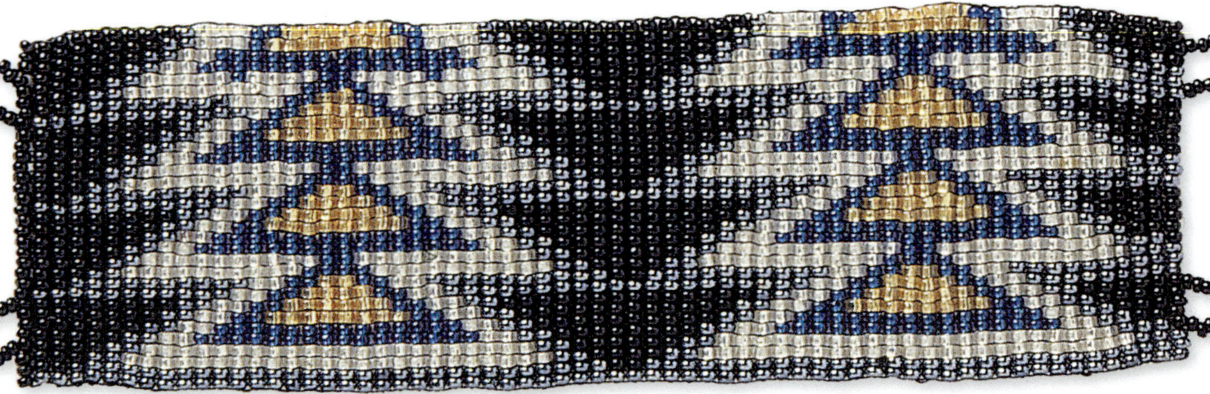

Arrowheads - Beads (Gunmetal, Black, Clear Silver Lined, Royal Blue Transparent, Clear Gold Silver Lined)
Prepare loom with 33 strands of Black thread (32 beads).

Snakes - Beads (Brown Transparent, Clear Silver Lined, Black, Teal Iridescent) **Prepare loom** with 33 strands of Black thread (32 beads).

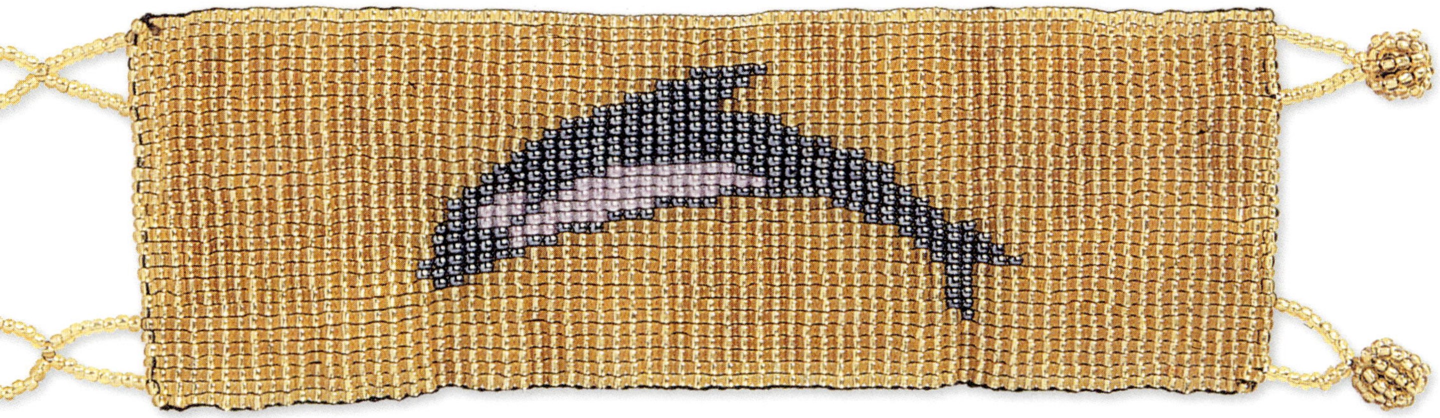

Dolphin - Beads (Clear Gold Silver Lined, Gunmetal, Clear Pink Lined) **Prepare loom** with 32 strands of Black thread (31 beads).

Mask - Beads (Black, Clear Pink Lined, Clear Gold Silver Lined, Royal Blue Silver Lined, Clear Silver Lined, Gunmetal, Green Silver Lined, Brown Transparent) **Prepare loom** with 33 strands of Black thread (32 beads).

Elegant Wide Bracelets ... 32 Beads Wide

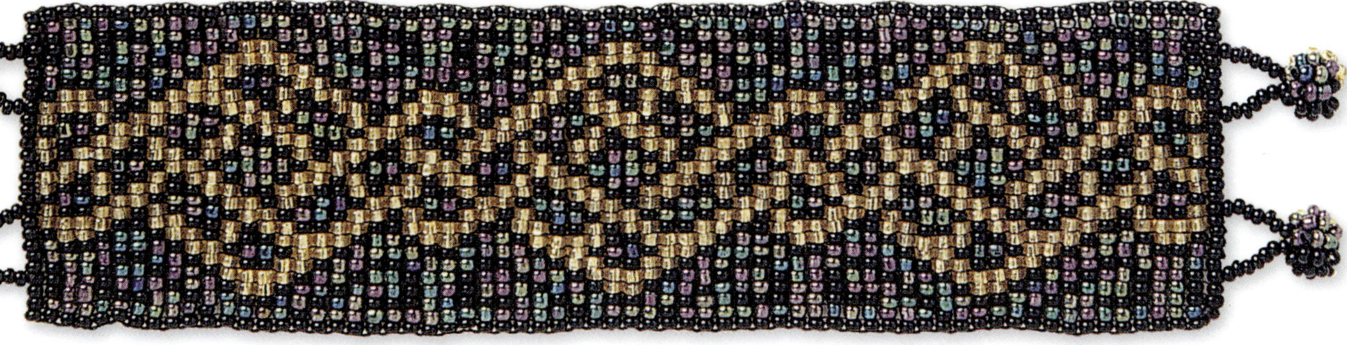

Celtic Knots - Beads (Black, Pink Iridescent, Blue Iridescent, Clear Gold Silver Lined) **Prepare loom** with 28 strands of Black thread (27 beads).

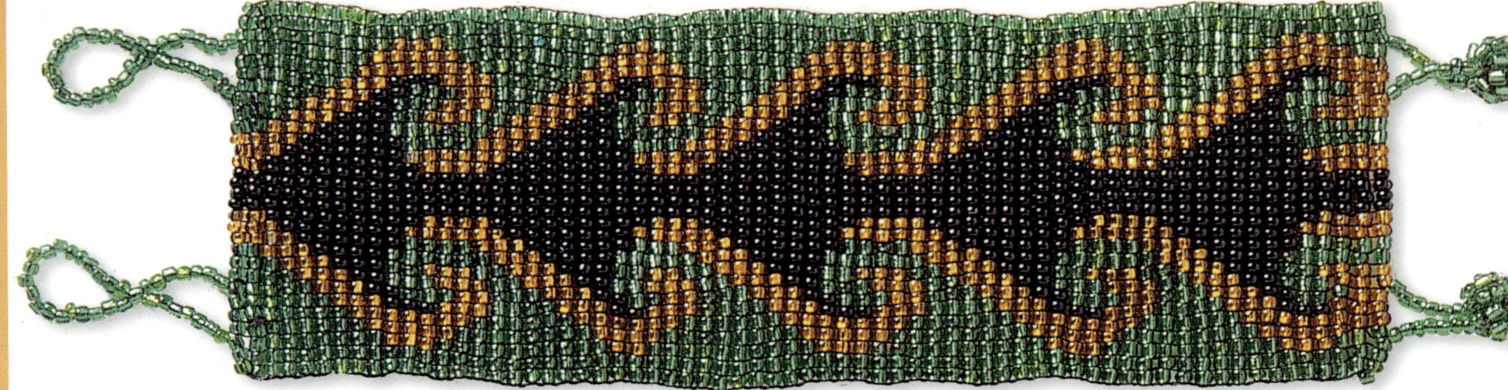

Stacked Urns - Beads (Green Silver Lined, Dark Clear Gold Silver Lined, Black) **Prepare loom** with 31 strands of Black thread (30 beads).

Green Hearts - Beads (Black, Dark Green, Lime Green, Lime Green Silver Lined, Green Silver Lined)
Prepare loom with 33 strands of Black thread (32 beads).

Diamond Lines - Beads (Black, Royal Blue Silver Lined, Lavender Pearl, Lime Green Silver Lined, Clear Green Lined, Clear Peach Lined, Clear Silver Lined, Clear Gold Silver Lined) **Prepare loom** with 33 strands of Black thread (32 beads).

Snowflakes - Beads (Black, Green Silver Lined, Clear White Lined, Clear Pink Lined, Clear Gold Silver Lined, Clear Peach Lined)
Prepare loom with 33 strands of Black thread (32 beads).

Elegant Wide Bracelets ... 30 to 32 Beads

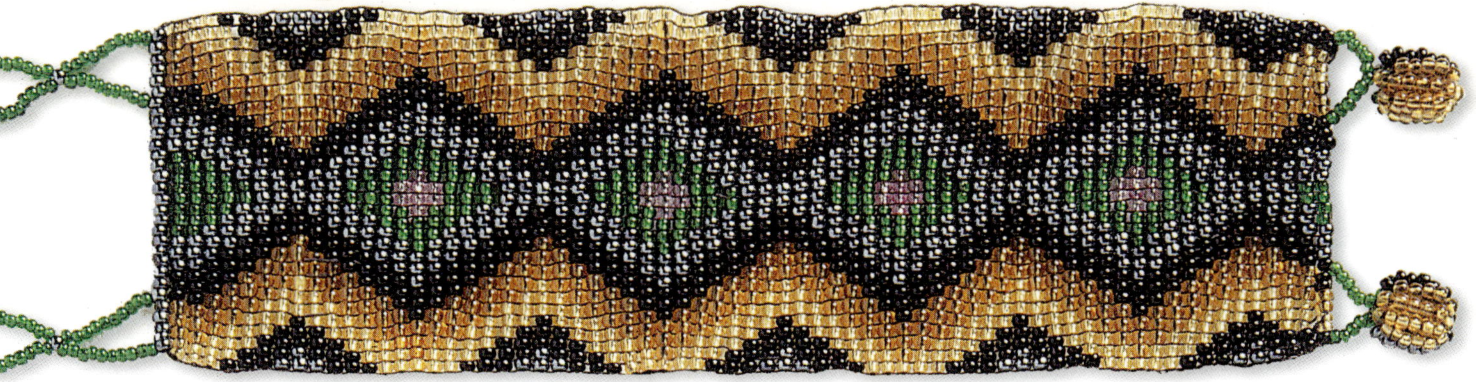

Diamond Path - Beads (Gunmetal, Black, Clear Gold Silver Lined, Dark Clear Gold Silver Lined, Green Silver Lined, Pink Transparent)
Prepare loom with 31 strands of Black thread (30 beads).

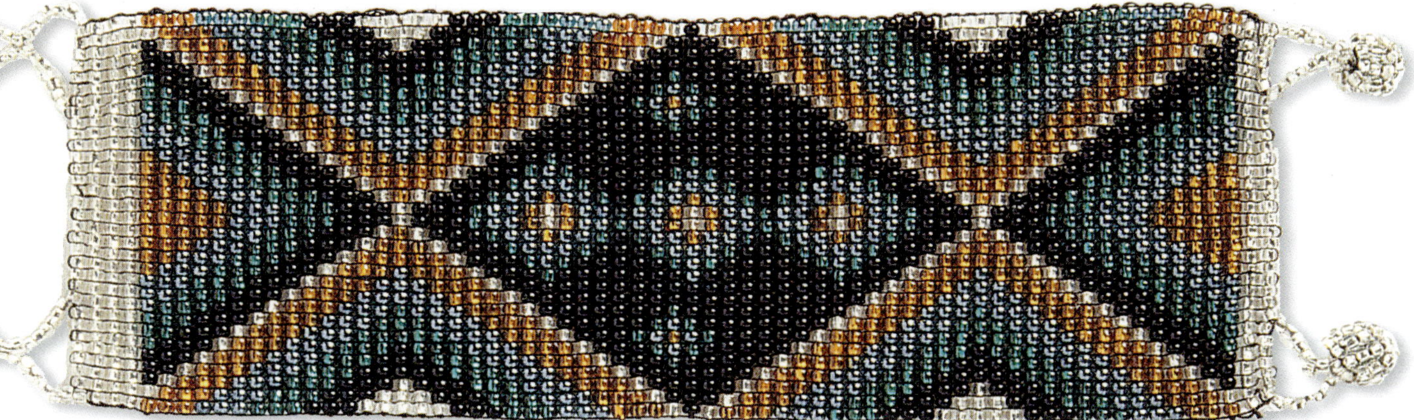

Diamond Rug - Beads (Clear Silver Lined, Clear Dark Gold Silver Lined, Clear Teal Iridescent, Teal Silver Lined, Black)
Prepare loom with 33 strands of Black thread (32 beads).

Diamond Path 2 - Beads (Black, Clear Purple Iridescent, Green Silver Lined, Clear Orange Iridescent, Gray Pearl, Clear Sky Blue Lined)
Prepare loom with 33 strands of Black thread (32 beads).

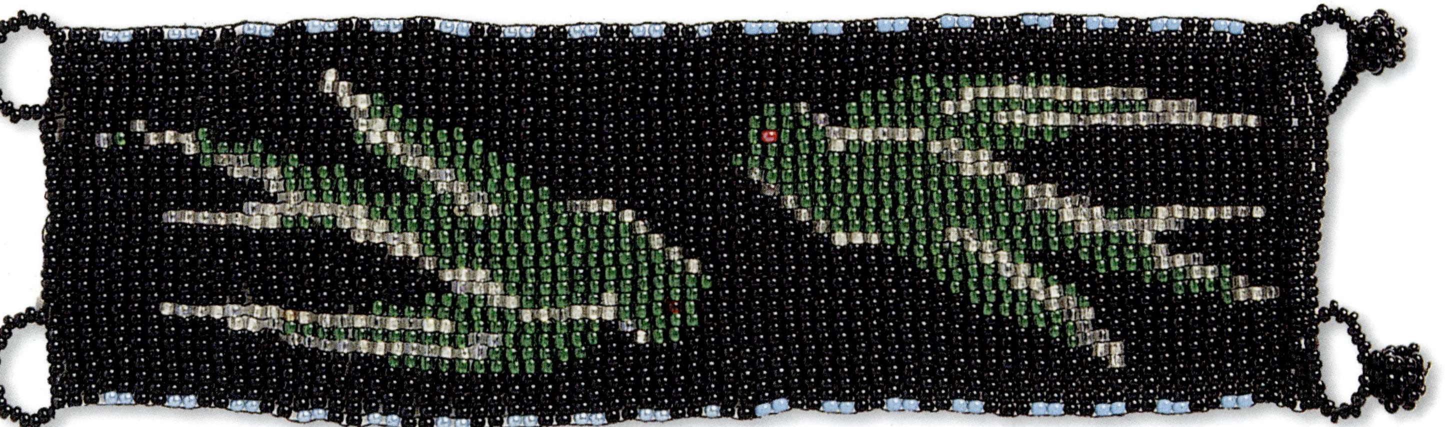

Swallows - Beads (Black, Sky Blue Pearl, Clear Silver Lined, Green Silver Lined, Red) **Prepare loom** with 34 strands of Black thread (33 beads).

Bracelets ... 30 to 32 Beads Wide

Four Diamonds - Beads (Black, Yellow, Green Silver Lined, Red Silver Lined) **Prepare loom** with 33 strands of Black thread (32 beads).

Yellow Urns - Beads (Black, Yellow, Green Silver Lined, Red Silver Lined) **Prepare loom** with 33 strands of Black thread (32 beads).

Primary Diamonds - Beads (Black, Yellow, Green Silver Lined, Red Silver Lined) **Prepare loom** with 33 strands of Black thread (32 beads).

Center Motif - Beads (Black, Yellow, Green Silver Lined, Red Silver Lined) **Prepare loom** with 33 strands of Black thread (32 beads).

Woven Diamonds - Beads (Black, Yellow, Green Silver Lined, Red Silver Lined) **Prepare loom** with 33 strands of Black thread (32 beads).

Stained Glass - Beads (Black, Yellow, Green Silver Lined, Red Silver Lined) **Prepare loom** with 33 strands of Black thread (32 beads).

Twin Zags - Beads (Black, Yellow, Green Silver Lined, Red Silver Lined) **Prepare loom** with 33 strands of Black thread (32 beads).

Triple Diamonds - Beads (Black, Yellow, Green Silver Lined, Red Silver Lined) **Prepare loom** with 33 strands of Black thread (32 beads).

Aqua Fantasy - Seed Beads (Black, Black Iridescent, Clear Pink Lined), 5mm Clear Aqua Silver Lined twisted bugle beads
Prepare loom with 8 strands of Black thread (7 beads - 1 seed, 1 bugle, 3 seed, 1 bugle, 1 seed).

Green Diamonds - Seed Beads (Clear White Lined, Black, Green Silver Lined), 5mm Clear Green Silver Lined bugle beads
Prepare loom with 14 strands of Black thread (11 beads - 1 seed, 1 bugle, 7 seed, 1 bugle, 1 seed).

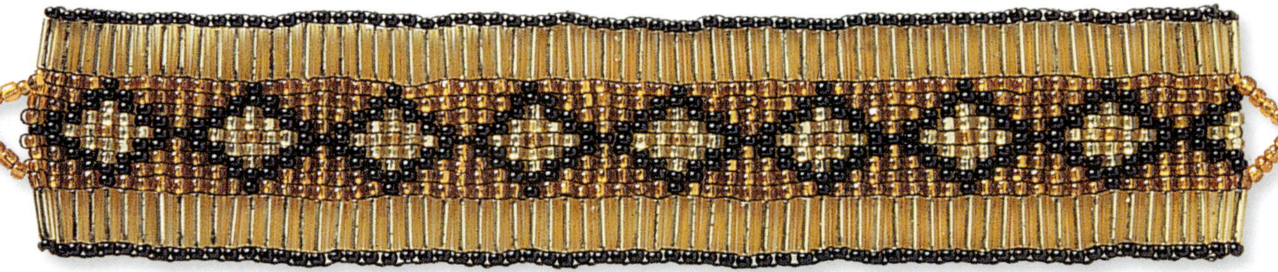

Gold Diamonds - Seed Beads (Clear Dark Gold Silver Lined, Black, Clear Gold Silver Lined), 5mm Clear Gold Silver Lined bugle beads
Prepare loom with 14 strands of Black thread (13 beads - 1 seed, 1 bugle, 9 seed, 1 bugle, 1 seed).

Blue Triangles - Seed Beads (Royal Blue Silver Lined, Black, Clear Gold Silver Lined), 5mm Clear Silver Lined bugle beads
Prepare loom with 14 strands of Black thread (13 beads - 1 seed, 1 bugle, 9 seed, 1 bugle, 1 seed).

Blue & White - Seed Beads (Clear White Lined, Royal Blue Silver Lined, Clear Gold Silver Lined), 5mm Clear Blue Silver Lined bugle beads
Prepare loom with 14 strands of Black thread (13 beads - 1 seed, 1 bugle, 9 seed, 1 bugle, 1 seed).

Diagonals - Seed Beads (Clear Yellow Lined, Blue Iridescent, Clear Hot Pink Lined, Lavender Pearl), 5mm Clear Royal Blue Silver Lined bugle beads
Prepare loom with 14 strands of Black thread (13 beads - 1 seed, 1 bugle, 9 seed, 1 bugle, 1 seed).

Bugle Beads

You'll love these bracelets... longer bugle beads weave up faster than seed beads.

TIP - As you work, check bugle beads for broken ends which will cut your thread. Discard any bugle beads that are broken.

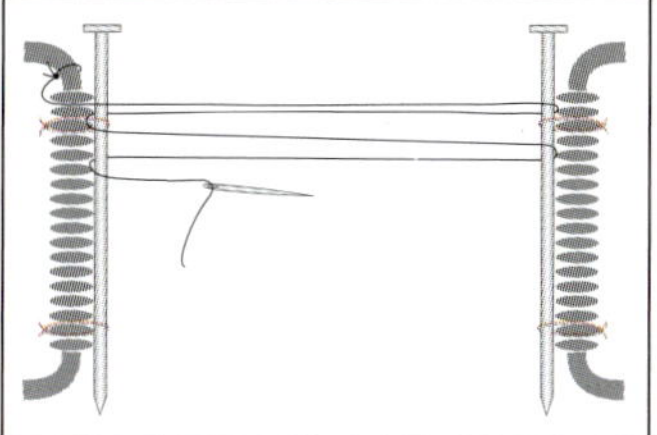

1. Warp loom as usual, but you must leave enough space for the bugle beds.

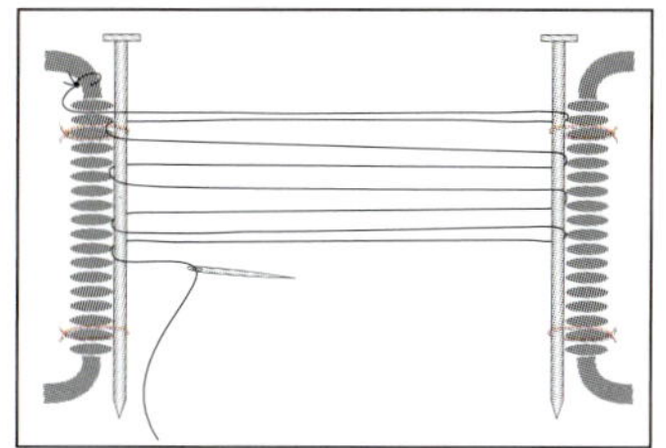

2. Begin beading, with thread going UNDER warp threads. Move threads in place with the needle.

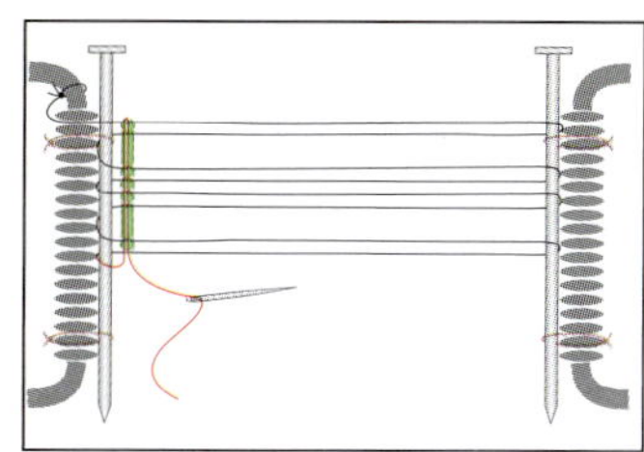

3. Pass needle back thru beads, going OVER warp threads. After 1st row, warp threads will be in position.

Bracelets with Bugle Beads ... Quick & Fun!

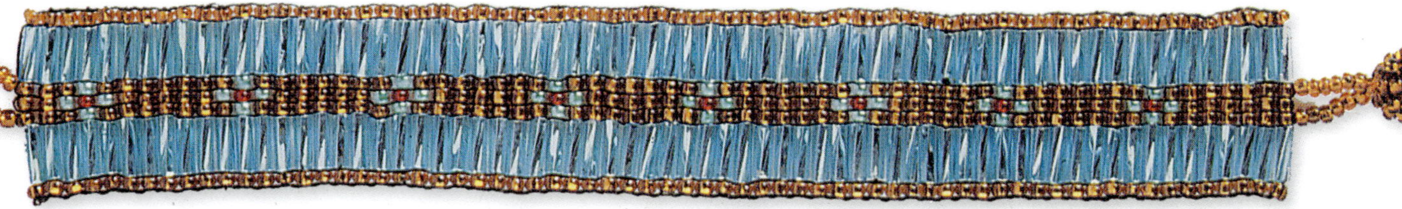

Aqua & Gold - Seed Beads (Brown Silver Lined, Clear Aqua Lined, Red Silver Lined), 5mm Clear Aqua Silver Lined twisted bugle beads
Prepare loom with 8 strands of Black thread (7 beads - 1 seed, 1 bugle, 3 seed, 1 bugle, 1 seed).

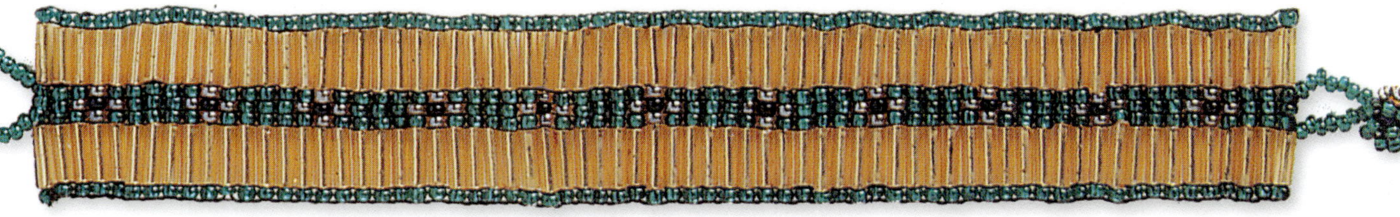

Green & Gold - Seed Beads (Green Silver Lined, Clear Orange Iridescent, Black), 5mm Clear Gold Silver Lined bugle beads
Prepare loom with 8 strands of Black thread (7 beads - 1 seed, 1 bugle, 3 seed, 1 bugle, 1 seed).

Green Points - Lime Green Transparent seed beads, 5mm Clear Lime Green Silver Lined bugle beads
Prepare loom with 7 strands of White thread (6 beads - 1 seed, 4 bugle, 1 seed).
Add picot points on the edges for a lacey look.

Add Edges

Use seed beads to add a fun beaded picot edge on any bracelet. This technique creates a lacy feminine effect.

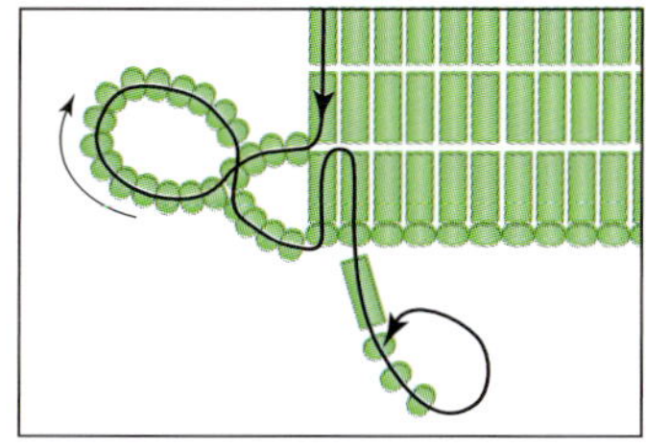

1. Thread on 1 bugle bead and 3 seed beads.

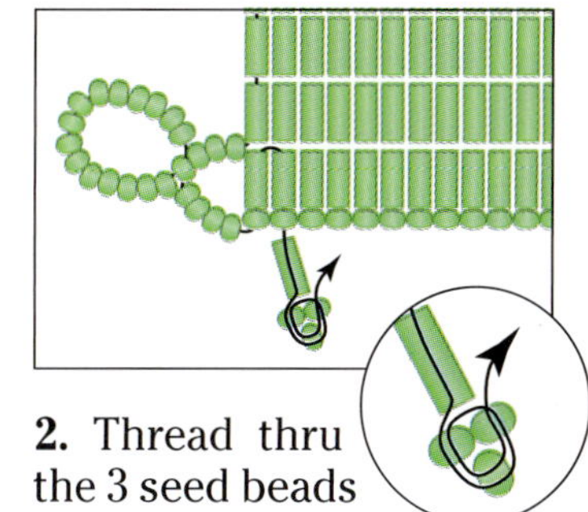

2. Thread thru the 3 seed beads again.

3. Add another bugle bead. Skip 2 beads, go thru 2 beads on the edge then repeat steps 1 thru 3.

Elegant Diamond - Seed Beads (Clear Pink Lined, Green Silver Lined, Clear Gold Silver Lined, Blue Iridescent, Clear Orange Iridescent, Pink Iridescent, Clear Silver Lined), 5mm Blue Iridescent bugle beads
Prepare loom with 24 strands of White thread (23 beads - 1 seed, 1 bugle, 9 seed, 1 bugle, 9 seed, 1 bugle, 1 seed).

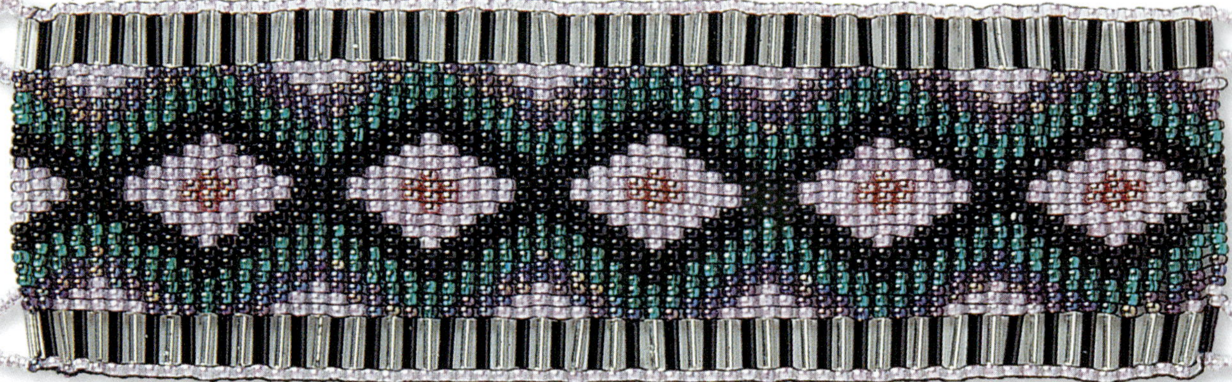

Pink Diamonds - Seed Beads (Clear Pink Lined, Purple Iridescent, Teal Silver Lined, Black, Red Transparent), 5mm Bugle Beads (Black, Clear Silver Lined) **Prepare loom** with 27 strands of Black thread (26 beads - 1 seed, 1 bugle, 22 seed, 1 bugle, 1 seed).

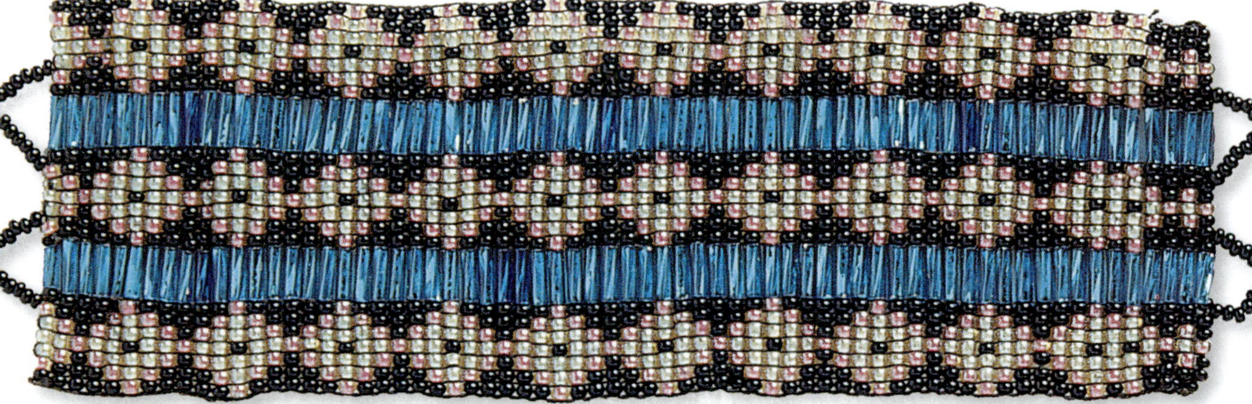

Tiny Diamonds - Seed Beads (Black, Clear Pink Lined, Clear Lime Green Lined), 5mm Clear Aqua Silver Lined twisted bugle beads
Prepare loom with 24 strands of Black thread (23 beads - 7 seed, 1 bugle, 7 seed, 1 bugle, 7 seed).

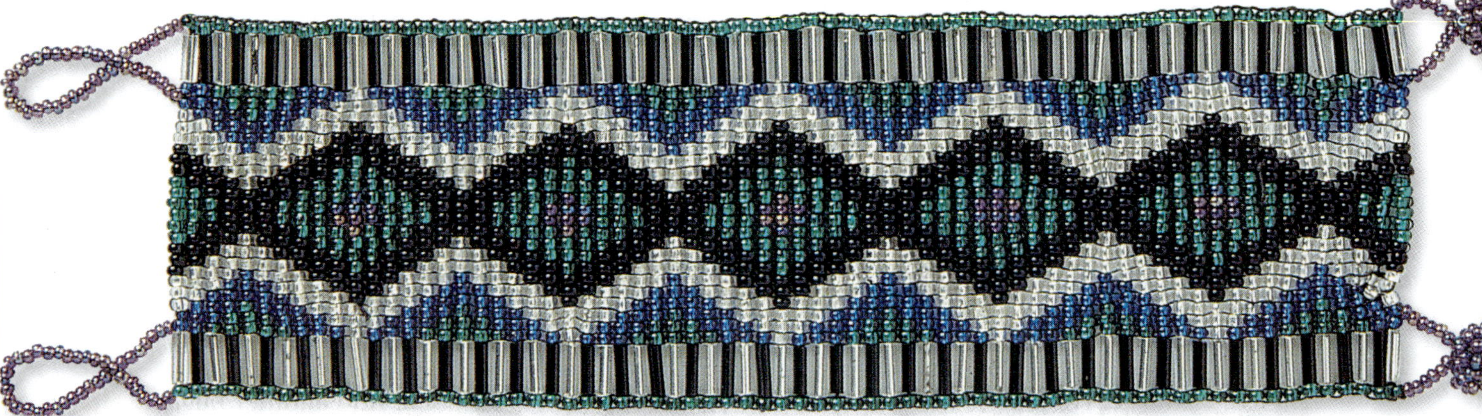

Green Diamonds - Seed Beads (Royal Blue Silver Lined, Teal Silver Lined, Clear Silver Lined, Black, Clear Purple Iridescent), 5mm Bugle Beads (Black, Clear Silver Lined) **Prepare loom** with 27 strands of Black thread (26 beads - 1 seed, 1 bugle, 22 seed, 1 bugle, 1 seed).

Bracelets with Bugle Beads ... Quick & Fun!

Blue Butterflies - Seed Beads (Clear Teal Iridescent, Black, Clear Green Lined, Green Silver Lined, Lavender Pearl, Red Transparent), 5mm Royal Blue Silver Lined bugle beads **Prepare loom** with 27 strands of Black thread (26 beads - 1 seed, 1 bugle, 22 seed, 1 bugle, 1 seed).

Three Orange Flowers - Seed Beads (Black, Green Silver Lined, Orange Iridescent, Clear White Lined, Blue Transparent), 5mm Clear Blue Silver Lined bugle beads **Prepare loom** with 25 strands of Black thread (24 beads - 1 seed, 1 bugle, 20 seed, 1 bugle, 1 seed).

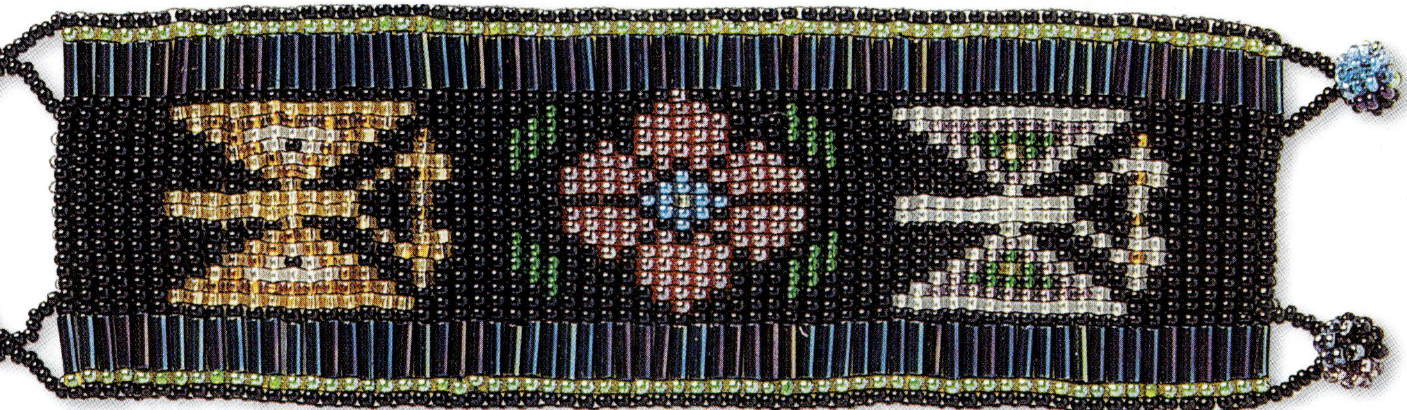

Butterflies & Flower - Seed Beads (Black, Clear Gold Silver Lined, Brown Silver Lined, Clear Silver Lined, Green Silver Lined, Clear Red Iridescent, Clear Turquoise Silver Lined, Mauve Silver Lined, Clear Lime Green Silver Lined), 5mm Blue Iridescent bugle beads **Prepare loom** with 25 strands of Black thread (24 beads - 2 seed, 1 bugle, 18 seed, 1 bugle, 2 seed).

Jewel Rows - Seed Beads (Black, Clear Red Iridescent), 5mm Bugle Beads (Clear, Blue Silver Lined twisted, Clear Lime Green Silver Lined) **Prepare loom** with 15 strands of Black thread (14 beads - 1 seed, 1 bugle, 1 seed, 1 bugle, 6 seed, 1 bugle, 1 seed, 1 bugle, 1 seed).

Wavy Line

It is easy to add a wavy line or 'vine' on top of any loom bracelet. Simply add strings of seed beads to the surface.

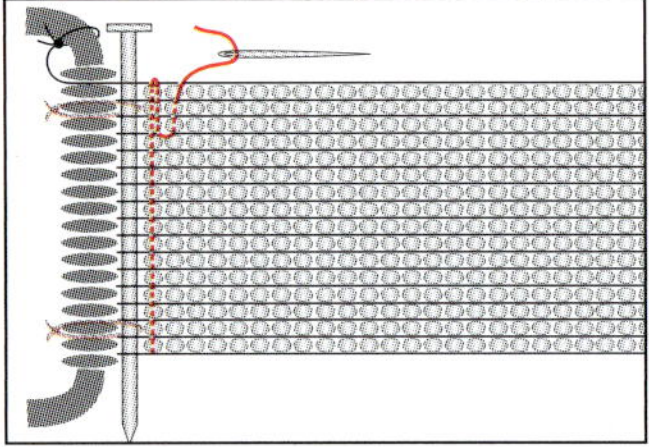

1. Weave a bracelet as usual. Take thread back thru two rows, bring needle up out of bracelet.

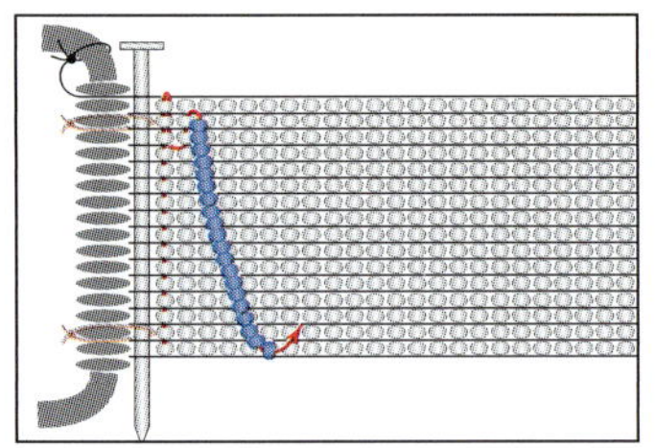

2. Add enough vine beads to angle across the bracelet as shown.

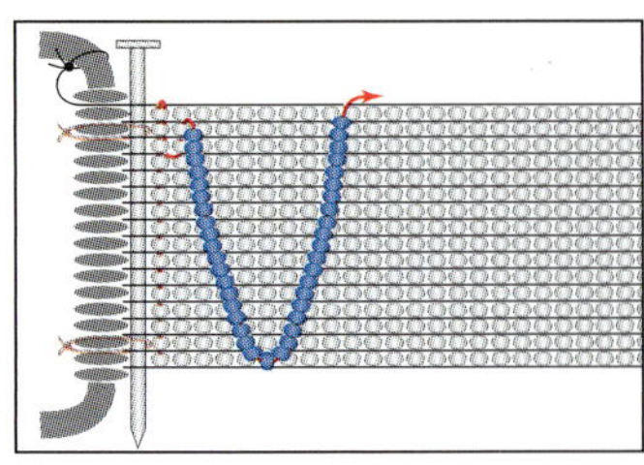

3. Thread back thru a bead on the opposite side of the bracelet. Repeat to the end of bracelet.

Make a Flower

Create little daisy type flowers on top of any loom bracelet. They add a touch of texture and they add extra color.

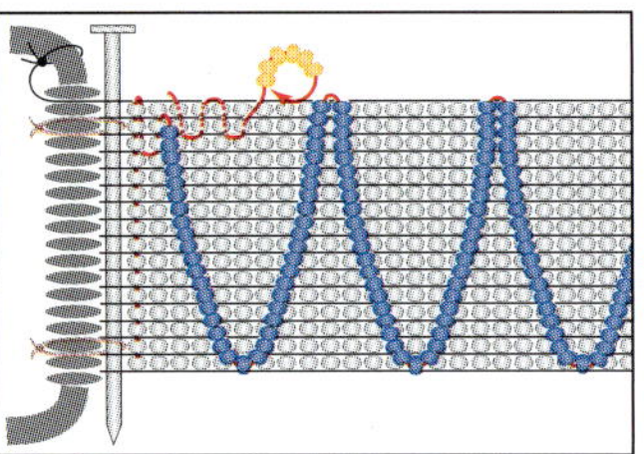

1. Pass thread back thru the vine to beginning (for added strength). Work thread thru beads for three rows, bring needle out of bracelet. Add 6 beads for flower.

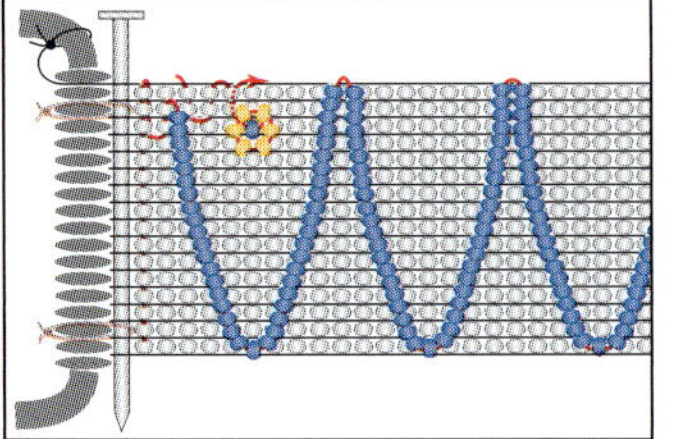

2. Go back thru beads just added to make a circle. Bring needle out of circle, add bead for center of flower, go back thru a few beads in a circle. (See page 19, diagrams 1-3.)

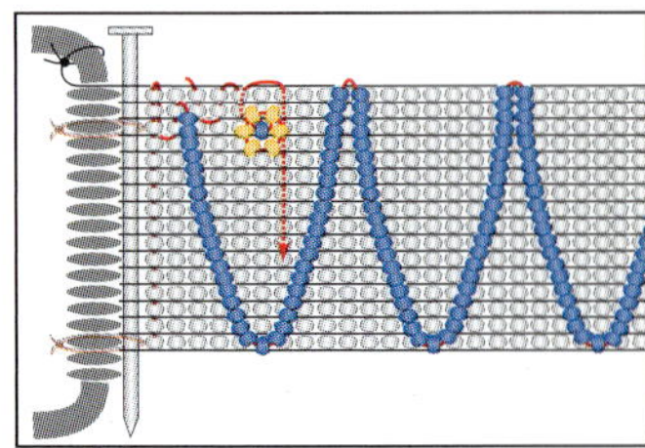

3. Work thread back thru bracelet beads to the next flower spot. Repeat, adding flowers as shown. Tie thread off.

Flower Garden Bracelets ... 16 Beads Wide

Red Flowers - Beads (Black, Clear Red Silver Lined, Assorted Opaque, Lined and Transparent for flowers)
Prepare loom with 17 strands of Black thread (16 beads).

White Flowers - Beads (Blue Iridescent, Clear White Lined, Assorted Opaque, Lined and Transparent for flowers)
Prepare loom with 17 strands of White thread (16 beads).

Green Flowers - Beads (Green Silver Lined, Assorted Opaque, Lined and Transparent for flowers)
Prepare loom with 17 strands of Black thread (16 beads).

Add Jewels between the Blocks of seed beads

Extra time and attention in warping the loom is the secret to these designs.

What great results with sparkling jewels between the blocks.

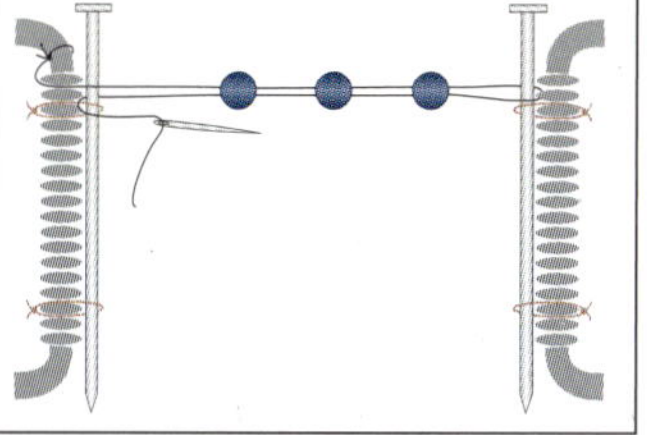

1. Begin to warp as usual, but add 3 jewel beads to the first thread. Continue with three more warp threads, passing the needle thru the beads on the first thread.

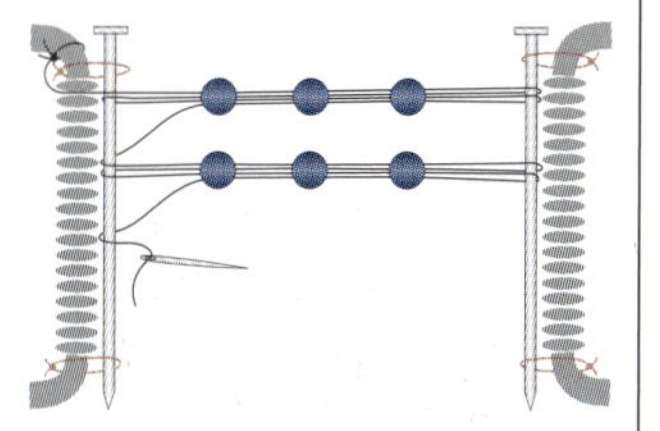

2. Thread 3 jewel beads onto the fifth thread. Pass the needle thru the second set of beads with the next three warp threads.

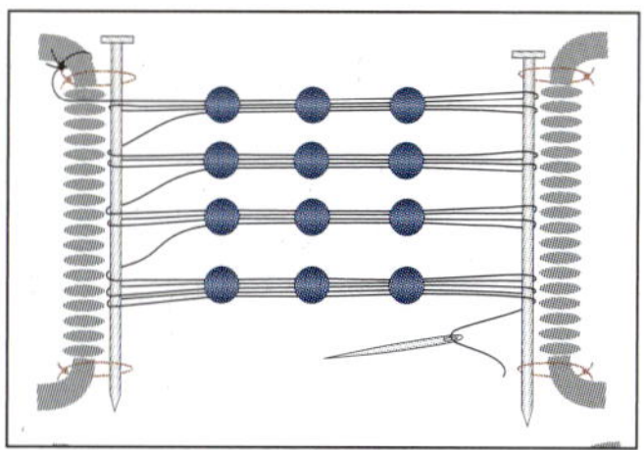

3. The third set of jewel beads will have 4 warp threads. Your last set of jewel beads will have 5 warp threads.

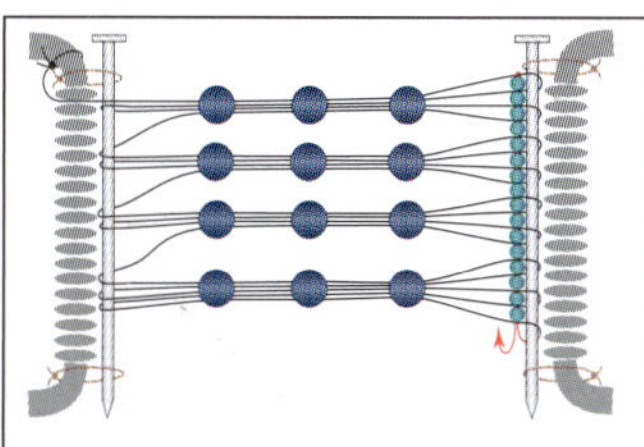

4. Begin beading as usual, using the needle to position warp threads on the first row.

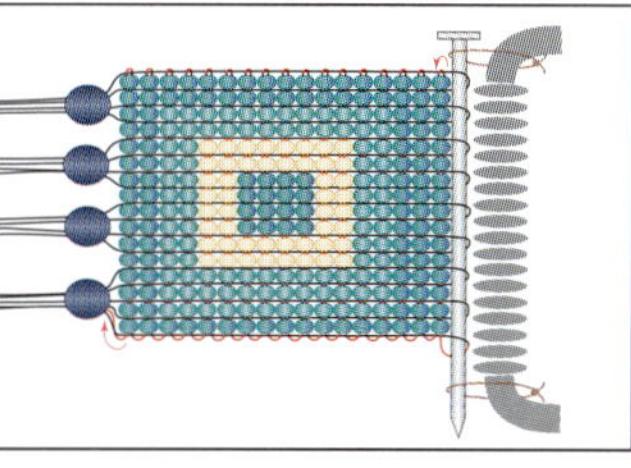

5. When you have completed the design section, push the first row of jewel beads against the beaded section.

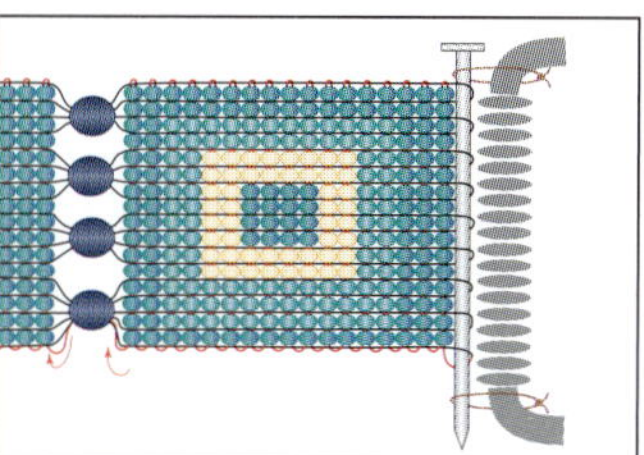

6. Pass the needle thru the closest jewel bead and continue beading.

Jeweled Bracelets ... 15 to 16 Beads Wide

Black Rectangles - Seed Beads (Black, Gunmetal, Clear Gold Silver Lined, Clear Dark Gold Silver Lined), 5mm jewel Mauve beads
Prepare loom with 17 strands of Black thread (16 beads).

Green Rectangles - Seed Beads (Clear Teal Iridescent, Green Silver Lined, Clear Cream Lined), 5mm jewel Black Iridescent faceted beads
Prepare loom with 17 strands of Black thread (16 beads).

Gold Diamonds - Seed Beads (Clear Pink Iridescent, Black, Clear Gold Silver Lined, Gunmetal), 5mm jewel Gold Transparent beads
Prepare loom with 16 strands of Black thread (15 beads).

Beautiful Bracelets ... For Every Occasion!

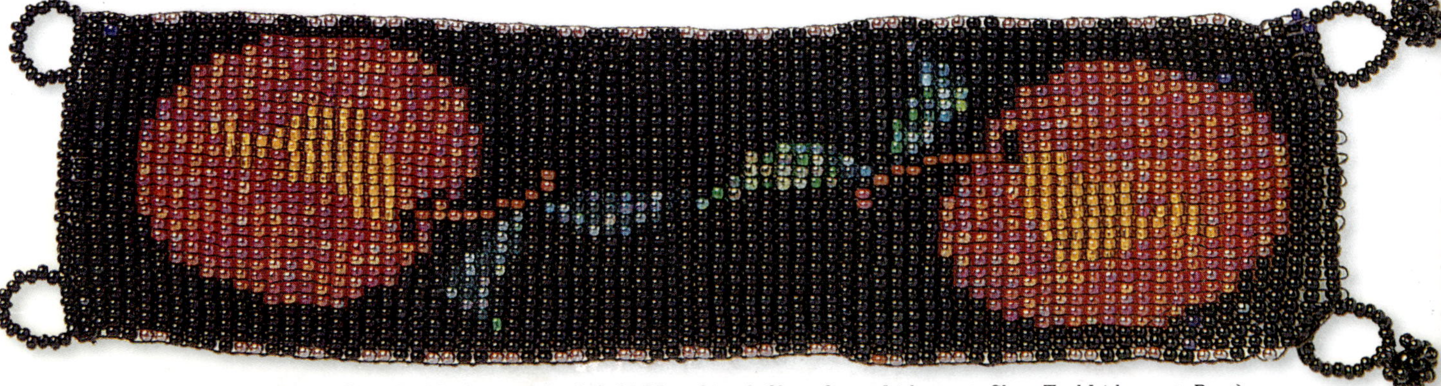

Apples - Beads (Black, Clear Red Iridescent, Dark Gold Silver Lined, Clear Green Iridescent, Clear Teal Iridescent, Rust) **Prepare loom** with 33 strands of Black thread (32 beads).

Flower Vases - Beads (Black, Turquoise, Lime Green, Clear Silver Lined, Red Transparent, Pink Pearl, Yellow, White Pearl, Brown Transparent, Royal Blue, Gold Silver Lined, Mauve Silver Lined, Clear Iridescent) **Prepare loom** with 33 strands of Black thread (32 beads).

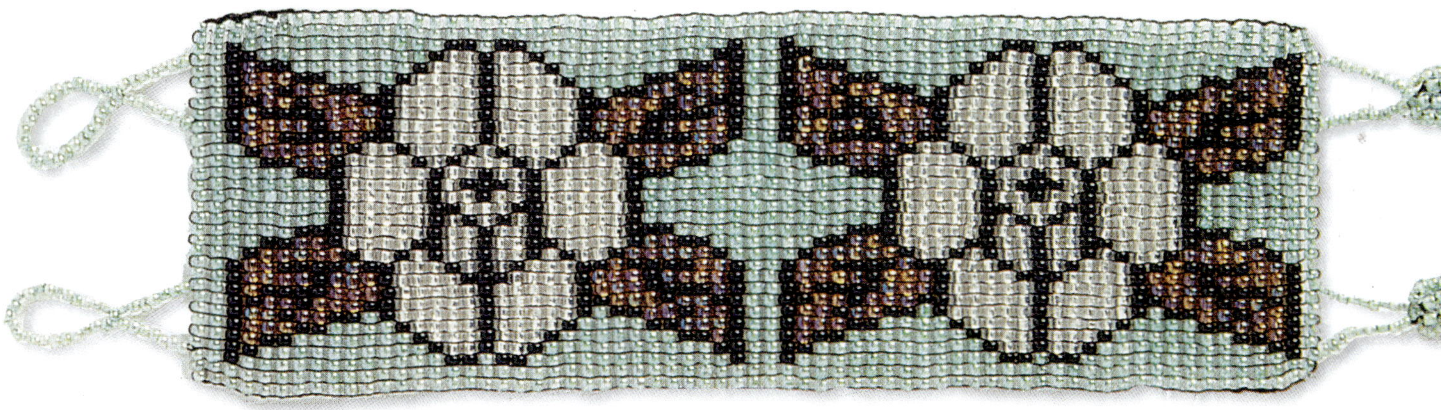

Flower - Beads (Clear Green Lined, Black, Brown Iridescent, Clear Silver Lined) **Prepare loom** with 33 strands of Black thread (32 beads).

Diamond Patchwork - Beads (Dark Green, Dark Gold Silver Lined, Blue Iridescent, Red Iridescent, Green Silver Lined, Pink Silver Lined, Blue Pearl) **Prepare loom** with 33 strands of Black thread (32 beads).